MASTERING
ONLINE GEN

Volume I of Quillen's Essentials of Genealogy

www.essentialgenealogy.com

PRAISE FOR DAN'S BOOKS

"*Mastering Online Genealogy* written by W. Daniel Quillen is a great little book packed full of helpful tips in doing online family research ... This informative book has some great tips for beginners, as well as those who have been doing research for a while ... I look forward to reading all of the books in this genealogical series." – *Tina Sansone, Bella Online book review*

"*Mastering Online Genealogy* gives the essentials of basic genealogy. Using the principles the author outlines, a user should be able to get a "fast start" on tracing their family history. This is not an encyclopedia of all things genealogy, but rather a concise and easy read text with practical suggestions ... I found the author's examples of his personal experiences enlightening and novel." – *Mary J. Lohr*

"*Mastering Online Genealogy* is well written, very readable, made interesting and more relevant with examples of the author's own tree. Excellent book for beginners, but also helpful for those with more experience in that it reminds you of correct methods, great resources and common pitfalls." – *luvourdog commenting on the Kindle edition*

"... It is not only informative but entertaining. Incorporating your own experiences in brought the book to life. Again, thank you for helping me to understand the many aspects of genealogy and for supplying a roadmap to finding more information about our ancestors." – *Dana L. Hager*

"Of all the books I have looked at yours is the best...and you write with your heart and soul. Thanks for writing such a great book." – *Karen Dredge*

"I got this book out of the library, but before I was half-way through it, I decided I had to have my own copy. Lots of helpful suggestions! I'd recommend it for all new and experienced family historians." – *Margaret Combs*

"I am embarking on the family history journey and have found your book to be very helpful ... thanks for putting together a helpful, easy to follow guide." – *Suzanne Adams*

"I'm absolutely delighted that I discovered your book *Secrets of Tracing Your Ancestors*. I've only been at this for a month (to keep sane during knee surgery recuperation) and now I'm hooked." – *Cecily Bishop*

About the Author

For more than 20 years, W. Daniel Quillen has been a professional writer specializing in travel and technical subjects. He has taught beginning genealogy courses to university students and working adults, and is a frequent lecturer in beginning and intermediate genealogy classes in Colorado. He has compiled his years of genealogical training and research into a growing series of genealogy how-to books. He lives in Centennial, Colorado with his wife and children. If you would like to contact Dan about anything in this book, his e-mail address is: **wdanielquillen@gmail.com**.

MASTERING ONLINE GENEALOGY

Volume I of Quillen's Essentials of Genealogy

www.essentialgenealogy.com

W. Daniel Quillen

Author of *Secrets of Tracing Your Ancestors*; *The Troubleshooter's Guide to Do-It-Yourself Genealogy*; and Quillen's Essentials of Genealogy primers

Cold Spring Press

COLD SPRING PRESS
www.essentialgenealogy.com

This 2015 edition printed for Barnes & Noble, Inc.

ISBN 13: 978-159360-208-6

Printed in the United States of America

PHOTO CREDITS

Cover design by Matthew Simmons (www.myselfincluded.com). Front cover photos from istockphoto.com. Back cover photo of family from flickr.com by Greene Connections. Photo on page 7 from flickr.com by T"eresa. Photo on page 71 from flickr.com by robfromamersfoort. Photo on pages 72, 90, and 144 from flickr.com by Greene Connections. Photos on pages 74, 100 (top), and 131 (top) from W. Daniel Quillen. Photo on page 100 (bottom) from from flickr.com by Cat Sidh. Photo on page 131 (bottom) from from flickr.com by cunningba.

If you want to contact the author directly, e-mail him at: wdanielquillen@gmail.com

TABLE OF CONTENTS

2662

1. INTRODUCTION

Welcome to the world of online genealogy! Whether you have been working (playing!) in the world of genealogy for years and years, or this is the first book on how to do genealogy you have picked up, you should be able to learn some tricks of the trade through the pages of this book!

Mastering Online Genealogy will help you learn (or relearn, or practice) how to use one of the greatest tools for information research and location ever created: the Internet. Daily, thousands upon thousands of documents formerly available only by expensive and time-consuming personal visits to distant locations are coming online. As you learn the techniques and sources of information in this book, you'll be able to find and access these records in record time, and be able to find more and more of your ancestors.

Sometimes, the search will be easy – a piece of cake in common parlance. Other times it will take every ounce of detective skills you possess to ferret out elusive ancestors. Regardless of easy or hard, obvious or subtle, the journey will be exciting and the find exhilarating.

In addition to this book, which does a focused dive into the world of online genealogy, there are several other books that might help round out your understanding of the world of genealogy:

If you are a beginning genealogist, you might consider picking up a book I wrote specifically for beginning genealogists – *Secrets of Tracing Your*

Ancestors. *Secrets* will start you at the very beginning, with organization and where to find information close at hand, and then provides you with techniques and strategies for finding your ancestors. Reviewers have even observed that there are tactics and information in the book that are good for experienced genealogists as well.

If you are a more experienced genealogist, then you should consider picking up another of the genealogy books I have written: *Troubleshooter's Guide to Do-It-Yourself Genealogy*. It is targeted at those who have moved beyond the beginner's resources and are beginning to hit some real stumbling blocks in their research. It serves to provide you some sources you may not have been aware of, how to access them and how to get the most out of them.

Okay – now that we're past the shameless self-marketing, let's get on with this book.

As I have done in my previous books, I am going to introduce you to my family. Many of them have interesting stories unraveled only through online research, and I will use them to teach you various and sundry techniques and sources that you will be able to use to find your own difficult-to-track-down ancestors!

I am William Daniel Quillen, and I am married to the lovely Bonita Blau. We have six children.

My parents are:
William Edgar Quillen and Versie Lee Lowrance.

As you research, have in mind the surnames of other families your family married into!

My grandparents were:

- Helon Edgar Quillen and Vivian Iris Cunningham.
- Elzie Lee Lowrance and Alma Hudson.

My great grandparents were:

- Edgar Estil Quillen and Theodora Charity McCollough
- William Edward Cunningham and Emma Adelia Sellers
- Thomas Newton Lowrance and Margaret Ann McClure
- Francis Marion Hudson and Margaret Ellen Turpin

My 2nd great grandparents were:

- Jonathan Baldwin Quillen and Sarah Minerva Burke
- William Lindsay McCollough and Lucy Arabella Phillips
- William Huston Cunningham and Amanda Stunkard
- John Thomas Sellers and Celeste Elizabeth Horney
- Alpheus Marion Lowrance and Catherine Gemima Reece
- Jeremiah Hudson and Frances Duvall

My 3rd great grandparents were:

- Charles Franklin Quillen and Susan or Susannah __________
- Samuel McCollough and Elizabeth Throckmorton
- Oliver Sayers Phillips and Charity Graham
- Joseph Cunningham and Sarah Rogers
- Matthew Stunkard and Margaret Peoples
- John T. Sellers and Elizabeth Ritchey
- Leonidas Horney and Jane Crawford
- Francis Marion Hudson and Mary Magdalene Yates
- John E. Duvall, Jr. and Elizabeth ______________

As you may readily surmise from the above information, even as involved in genealogical research as I am, I have been unable to fill in the complete information for all my ancestors in just these few generations. Some lines I have traced back to medieval Ireland, and still others barely make it back to the 19th century. Doubtless you have the same kinds of ancestors: those who make it easy to find them, others who like to throw detours in your way, and still others who seemingly want nothing to do with your research efforts. Hopefully by the time you finish this book, you will have discovered techniques that will help you find even the most elusive of your ancestors!

So – if you're ready, let's jump right in!

Daniel Quillen
December 2014
"I seek dead people" (with apologies to *The Sixth Sense*!)

2. THE ESSENTIALS

The longest journey begins with a single step.
— attributed to Lao-Tzu (*c* 604-*c* 531 BC), founder of Taoism

Who am I to argue with Mr. Tzu? Perhaps this is the first step in your genealogical journey, or perhaps 10,000+ steps preceded it. If the latter is true, you'll know what follows in this chapter are the critical, essential steps to being a successful genealogist. If you are the former person – just taking your first steps in genealogy – learn the lessons in this chapter well or suffer the consequences! Many of them are in this book for the simple reason that I did not learn these lessons when I first started my genealogical journey, and I have had to retrace many of my steps to do penance for my headlong dash down the genealogical pike. I hope to save you some steps by pointing out first essential steps to you.

The Basics

To be a viable structure, every building needs to be built with a strong foundation, quality materials and using sound building principles. Your genealogy research needs the same features – a strong foundation, solid materials, sound building principles, etc. If you do not have those features, you are asking for trouble down your family line.

Following are a few of the basic building blocks and tools with which you'll want to work while building your genealogical house – the House of

Quillan, Hudson House, etc. This chapter is a bit of a free flow of consciousness. Not much rhyme or reason, but each snippet is an important one for you to remember and practice, lest you regret not having done so. Since this is a book on maximizing online genealogical resources, and these are mostly not about online sources (but important nonetheless), I have just shared the basics of the basics. As I mentioned earlier, if you want or need more on these topics, you can check out *Secrets of Tracing Your Ancestors.*

Notes

First – keep notes. Good notes. Write down the source of every scrap and tidbit of genealogical information about your ancestors that comes your way. Even if it's a family story told you by your great aunt Ruth, write it down and record the source. Record the titles of books. If you found the book in a library, include the call numbers and where the book was located. Include the page numbers.

If you've found information on the Internet, include not only the information but the URL of the website. Nothing is more frustrating than to have some great information in your notes about an ancestor, and you know it was from a website, and simply cannot recall what the name of the website is, much less the URL.

Keep good notes!
Record sources!

A few years ago I was poking around the Internet looking for my great-great grandfather, Jonathan Baldwin Quillen. We knew he was born someplace near the confluence of the states of Virginia, Kentucky, Tennessee and North Carolina. An older relative thought she heard he had been born in Hawkins County, Tennessee, so I figured that was a good place to search.

After a bit of searching, I found a genealogy society for Hawkins County, Tennessee. On the front page of the genealogy society, it listed the names of the society's members, and the surnames they were researching. Lo and behold, one of the members was doing research on Quillan / Quillen / Quillin family lines. I clicked on his name and was given his e-mail address. I immediately fired off an e-mail to him, then turned my attention to scouring the Internet again.

URL = abbreviation for *Universal Resource Locator.* Copy these down!

The next day, I thought I would see if I could find the website again. Nothing. No matter how creative I got, I was unable to find the website for that genealogy society again. To this day, I don't know where it went. Had I written down the URL (or simply cut-and-pasted it into my genealogy software), I could have found it in a heartbeat!

This was a good example of the reality that websites come up and go down all the time. They change names, service providers are changed resulting in a change of URL, etc.

Another good idea is to copy down the name of the owner / maintainer of the website – their names are usually listed along with their contact information and most often appear at the bottom of a web page. Occasionally their names appear in the *Contact Information* or *Contact Us* section. Had I done that with the Hawkins County genealogy society website, I could have contacted him / her to learn how to further access the site.

But don't worry about me – lucky for me (this time!), I had copied the e-mail address of the fellow who was researching the Quillen line. As you will later see, his information was a gold mine for me.

Be Specific

When you are contacting organizations and fellow genealogists, be specific in your requests. Don't make the mistake of saying:

"I am doing research on the Quillen family of Lee County, Virginia, and would like everything you have on that line."

That sort of a request will most likely yield a whole bunch of nothing, especially if you are contacting a government entity, like a county courthouse. A better – and probably a more successful – approach is to be specific in your request:

"I am doing research on my great-grandfather, Edgar Estil Quillen. I believe he was born in Lee County, Virginia on or about January 15, 1880 or 1881. His father was Jonathan Baldwin Quillen and his mother was Sarah Minerva Burke Quillen. I am seeking Edgar's birth certificate."

Or: "I am trying to locate the will of my great-great grandfather, Jonathan Baldwin Quillen. He died in Hartville, Wright County, Missouri on January 21, 1920."

Speed vs. Accuracy

When I do genealogy, like when I write, I always seem to have a tremendous sense of urgency. It seems as though I just can't get to information quickly enough, and when I find it, I seem compelled to record it as rapidly as possible. In so doing, I am chagrined to say, I have made far too many errors in recording dates, places, spellings of names, etc. Slow down, take your time, and record the information accurately about the individual you have found – the spelling of his name, her birth date and place, etc.

Standard Dating Format

This sounds simple, but get used to recording your dates as: day / month / year in the following format – DD/MM/YYYY. For example: 1 January 2011. Avoid the short cut of listing dates as 1/11/11. If you write a date in such a fashion, did you mean:

January 1, 2011? January 1, 1911? January 1, 1811??

Or: November 1, 2011? November 1, 1911? November 1, 1811?

The standard dating convention among genealogists is DD/MM (spelled out)/YYYY

Don't Give Up

Sometimes you will hit a brick wall. Every courthouse, every marriage record, birth registry, etc., just comes up empty for an ancestor you know was living in that town or county. Step back, take a deep breath, and maybe even turn your attention to someone else. New records are coming on line daily. What wasn't there today may be there tomorrow. Or next month. Or next year.

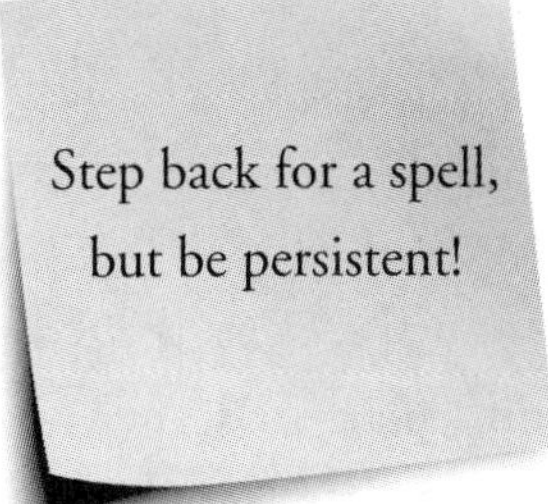
Step back for a spell,
but be persistent!

The key is not to give up completely. It's okay to set a research project aside for a time, but be sure and return to it and check if any new sources have become available that will shed light on your search.

The Journey

There are many ways of getting to where you're going in genealogy, and you have to learn what works best for you. If you don't mind, I'll liken your genealogical research to a journey, a journey to locate your ancestors.

What kind of a traveler are you? Are you the type that believes the shortest distance between two locations is a straight line? Do you jump on the highway, and get there as fast as you can? Or are you more of a meanderer?

Perhaps your research will take on your personal traveling characteristics. You may become so focused on a particular ancestor that you pass others by, others who, if you slowed down and looked around, might not only fill out your family tree, but might just lead you to the elusive ancestor on whom you were focused. Brothers, sisters, aunts, uncles, cousins, grandparents, etc., may yield results about your target ancestor through their wills (*I leave to my nephew Jonathan Baldwin Quillen...*), obituaries (*Priscilla Quillen Collingsworth is survived by two brothers, Jonathan of Hartville MO and Jimmy of Estilville, VA*), even society pages of old newspapers (*Mrs. Priscilla Collingsworth's brother Jonathan Quillen and his wife Sarah visited this week from their home in Hartville, Missouri.*) can yield additional, unknown information.

I know that through the years I have blasted past countless ancestors whose information was ripe for the picking, because I was so focused on another ancestor. Don't be so focused on one ancestor; slow down and enjoy the familial scenery that passes by as you pursue that ancestor who has been difficult to find, and you may find clues that will help you end the chase for the Elusive One.

But – **don't get lost in the trees!** Sometimes you can get so distracted following the thread of a trail for another ancestor that you completely lose track of the main purpose of your search – to find your great-great-grandfather's birth certificate. More than once I have found myself following leads like the thread that took me to my great-grandfather's son's wife's family. Yes, they are family – of a sort. Yes, I will probably want to capture their information some day. But if I spend hours and hours chasing and recording information about them, those are hours that I have been diverted from my true goal – the birth certificate of one of my progenitors.

Research Plan

To avoid getting lost in the woods (see above), especially if you find yourself to be one of those genealogists who take a lot of detours (I am guilty of this!) during your research, it might be really wise for you to develop a research plan. It can be as formal or as informal as you like. Handwritten or typed, detailed or high-level, whatever you find works best for you. At a minimum, here are some of the things that should go in your research plan:

Plan your work –
work your plan!

- The name of the person for whom you are searching
- The information you are seeking for that person – birth or death date, marriage date and / or spouse, death date, etc.
- Likely location
- Resources thought to be available

A Research Plan can be much, much more than this. It just depends on how detailed you want or need to get to keep you focused. When I research, my personal preference is not to have the journey laid out so perfectly that I miss some wonderful scenery along the way. Here's an easy, not-too-detailed research plan that has worked for me on many occasions. The details change based on names, locations, ancillary lines, etc.:

Research Goal	Find the birth date for Jonathan Baldwin Quillen
Probable location(s)	Sullivan Co, TN, Hawkins Co., TN, Hancock Co, TN, Lee Co., VA

Associated surnames	Burke (wife's maiden name)
Possible resources	Vital records for above counties, TN State Library & Archives, VA State Library & Archives, county genealogy society websites,
Comments	I have three dates for JB's birthdate: 18 May 1845, 21 May 1845, 17 September 1845.

Don't Procrastinate!

As you may have read in *Secrets of Tracing Your Ancestors*, every family seems to have that great aunt Ruth (or Uncle Charlie) who seems to have committed all the family stories, dates and places to memory. They are walking (or shuffling) Wiki's for your family genealogy. Do not wait to glean whatever information you can from these wonderful individuals. Unlike a website, once they are cached, their memories are no longer available for you to poke around in!

Seriously, one of the best sources for me as a genealogist – especially during the beginning generations of my own surname — through the years has been my great aunt Ruth. A widow living in rural Oklahoma all her life, she was the repository of all family history information in the family. She knew names, dates, and stories – why did great grandpa pick up the family and seemingly move overnight to Oklahoma from their native Virginia? Where was Aunt Agnes born, and wasn't her mother from Scotland?

I had the delight to meet with and interview her informally many times. But it wasn't enough. She is gone now, moved from her beloved Oklahoma to loftier spheres. I have tried picking the brains of her daughters, my great aunts, hoping that somehow that information exchange happened prior to Ruth's departure. But alas, the answer is almost always the same: "Oh, I don't know that. Mamma would have known that, but I just don't know. Sorry."

If you have such genealogy databanks still living, do NOT let them die before they have shared all they can.

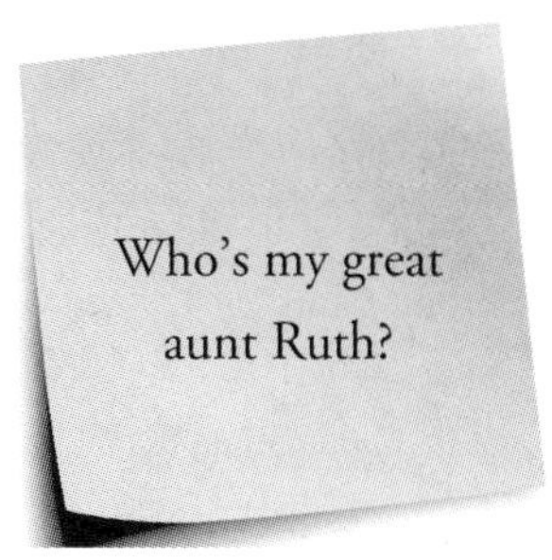

Primary and Secondary Sources

Let's have a brief discussion on *primary* and *secondary* sources of genealogical information. As a genealogist, your main goal should be to find primary sources of information on your ancestors whenever possible. Secondary sources are fine until you can find primary sources. *Hearsay* and *family legend* have their value, but their greatest genealogical value (next to entertainment and intrigue!) is in providing clues to finding primary and secondary sources of genealogical records. (They can, however, lead you astray for many years, so be careful how much weight you give them!)

Primary sources of genealogy information are those records that are created at the time of an event. An original birth certificate would be considered a primary source of information. An abstracted original birth certificate (information copied from an original many years after the fact) is valuable, but not as valuable as the original. *Birth* information on a *death* certificate would be considered a secondary source; *death* information on the *death* certificate would be considered a primary source.

What about the information found on census records? Would you consider that information as a primary or secondary source of information? With censuses becoming more and more available, that is a most important question. Based on my definitions of primary and secondary sources above, all vital records information (birth, death, marriage, etc.) found on census records are considered secondary sources.

To review:

Primary sources = good

Secondary sources = useful but not as good as a primary source

Hearsay / family legend = not so good (but interesting!)

Netiquette

Webster's Online Dictionary defines *netiquette* as: *etiquette governing use of the Internet.* Its only example cites the need not to use all capital letters in writing, as it makes you look like you are shouting So – DON'T SHOUT! I have a dear great aunt who e-mails occasionally. I don't know if she uses all caps because it makes it easier for her to see, but to my business-oriented brain, it comes across as shouting to me – and would to about anyone who uses e-mail in a business setting these days. My suggestion is that you use CAPS and **bolding** judiciously. Not to do so either ticks people off, or at least loses its ability to highlight important or critical information.

No **flaming**! Ever. Flaming is the practice of unloading your anger, disappointment, frustration, etc. on the recipient of the e-mail. If you encounter a particularly unhelpful clerk in a county court someplace, upon whose assistance you are completely and utterly dependent, if you unload on said person, I guarantee s/he will remember you the next time you need their services for an entirely different ancestor. Besides being unkind…. don't burn your bridges before you come to them.

Privacy Laws

I'll address privacy from several positions. First, there are laws governing the privacy of an individual's information. These should of course be adhered to. The government makes this easy on you as far as censuses go – they are not released until 72 years after the census enumeration date. (Yes, many genealogists are anxiously awaiting 2012 – the year the 1940 census will be available.)

In addition to legal restrictions on sharing information such as birth, marriage and death records, there are also common courtesies that should apply regarding privacy. Let me provide you with an example.

When I was beginning my genealogical journey, I became an early convert to the value and genealogic power of censuses. The plethora of information found there is exciting. I realized the information was almost all a secondary source, but it helped me visualize the families on whom I was doing research – and often enabled me to find primary sources. In particular, I had been thrilled to find my great grandfather and his family in several consecutive censuses. Francis Marion Hudson was known within the family as "Papa," and was reported to have ruled the roost with a bit of an iron fist — not abusive, just pretty much the situation of there being no question about who was the head honcho in the family. So strong was his influence that my grandmother had to sneak off to get married because Papa didn't approve of her sweetheart – my grandfather. After their marriage, they lived in Texas for years, away from the family, for fear of the consequences of returning to an unhappy Papa. Here are a couple of the census entries for my great grandfather:

Here Francis M. is as a rambunctious two-year-old in the Moreland Township, Pope County Arkansas 1880 census:

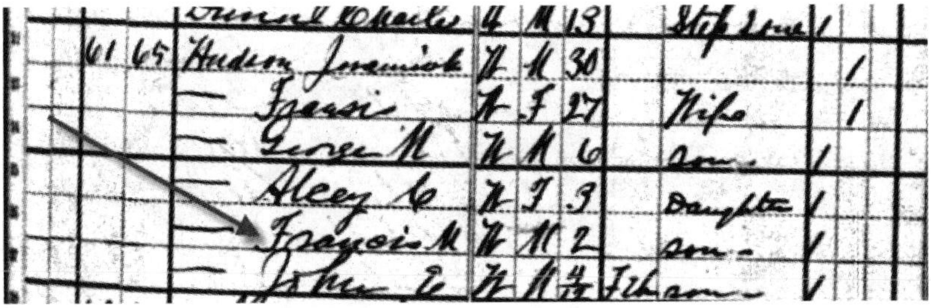

The 1890 census was lost in a fire, but here's my great grandfather in the 1900 census for Comanche, Oklahoma Indian Territory. He had apparently moved from his parents' home and was a 22-year-old laborer for James Martin:

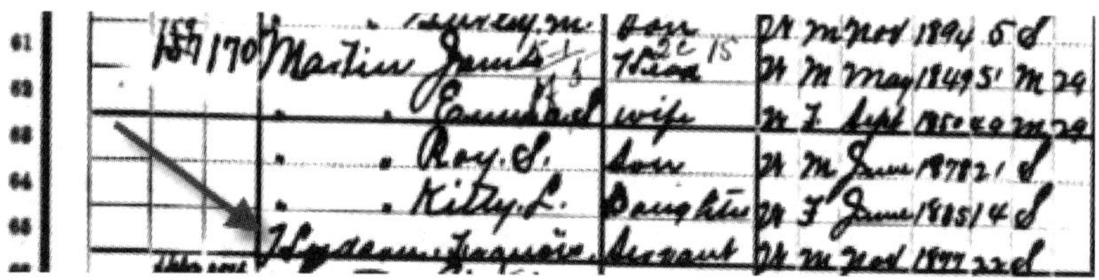

And here he is with his wife and a couple of brothers-in-law in the 1910 census for King Township, Stephens County, Oklahoma from the 1910 census. Note according to the census, he and his wife had been married less than a year (see the 0 listed in the column that says *Number of years of present marriage)*:

LOCATION.				NAME	RELATION.	PERSONAL DESCRIPTION.					Mother of how many children.	
Street, avenue, road, etc.	House number (in cities or towns).	Number of dwelling house in order of visitation.	Number of family in order of visitation.	of each person whose place of abode on April 15, 1910, was in this family. Enter surname first, then the given name and middle initial, if any. Include every person living on April 15, 1910. Omit children born since April 15, 1910.	Relationship of this person to the head of the family.	Sex.	Color or race.	Age at last birthday.	Whether single, married, widowed, or divorced.	Number of years of present marriage.	Number born.	Number now living.
		1	2	3	4	5	6	7	8	9	10	11
		122	124	Stroud, William R.	Head	M	W	31	M1	8		
				——, Julia	Wife	F	W	25	M1	8	4	4
				——, Annie May	Daughter	F	W	8	S			
				——, Ernest	Son	M	W	6	S			
				——, Lillie	Daughter	F	W	3	S			
		123	125	Earnhart, George Edward	Head	M	W	33	M2	5		
				——, Adaline	Wife	F	W	23	M1	5	1	1
				——, Jared	Son	M	W	4	S			
		124	126	Hudson, Francis M.	Head	M	W	30	M2	0		
				——, Maggie	Wife	F	W	21	M1	0		
				Turpen, James H.	Brother-in-law	M	W	35	D			
				——, Charley	Brother-in-law	M	W	31	S			
				——, Sylvester	Brother-in-law	M	W	16	S			

Whoa! This census indicated that my great grandfather had been married once before he married my great grandmother! (Note the M^2 in the *Whether single, married, widowed or divorced* column, indicating this was his second marriage!) This was news to me, and as far as I knew, to the rest of the family. I was concerned about how to handle this information, as I wasn't certain my grandmother, in particular, knew about this previous marriage of her father. I wasn't even sure my own mother was aware of this information.

My mother's sister, my aunt Carol, shares some of my interest in genealogy. It was she to whom I turned to check the information out. She confirmed the information, and even seemed to recall the name of my great grandfather's first wife. She recalled it had been marriage of young loves that didn't last even a year.

All that to say – be careful with the information you find that might be of a sensitive nature. More than one instance in my family history tells of out-of-wedlock births (or at least births within several months of marriage), divorces, illegal activity, etc.

3. WHAT COMPUTER SHALL I USE?

With apologies to Clement Clarke Moore:
"Now Acer! Now Gateway! Now Toshiba and Dell! On HP! On Big Blue!
On, Casio and Bell! From the top of my desk, to the Internet for all,
Now search away, search away, search away all!"

Since this book is about mastering online genealogy, I hope it is obvious you will need to use a computer to do that.

If you are like me, you are not very technically adept when it comes to computers. If that is the case, then this is a good chapter for you to peruse. If you're not like me, and you are technically adept, you have my permission to skip this chapter, guilt-free.

However, if you wish to read on in this chapter and evaluate my suggestions, please do so. If you have suggestions, I'd love to hear them, so e-mail me at the e-mail address listed in the front of this book.

For those who are computing-challenged, let's get back to computers. But before we do that, let's take a short detour and speak briefly about cars, since most of us are much more familiar with cars than we are with computers.

As of this writing, my wife and I own five cars (we have children...). We have two Fords, a Nissan, a Cadillac and a Saturn. Functionally, they are all pretty much the same. You get in, put your foot on the brake (and/or push the clutch in), turn the key and the engine starts. You put the car in gear and drive away. Pretty simple, and something we're all pretty familiar with.

So – which is the best car? It really depends on the task for which I am using the car. If I want good gas mileage, our Nissan Altima or Saturn are the best vehicles for us to use. But if I want to haul Boy Scouts on a camping trip over four-wheel drive roads, my Ford F150 extended cab is my best bet. If I am taking a long road trip and I am willing to sacrifice gas mileage for comfort, my 1995 Cadillac is the most comfortable ride we have. And finally, if I want to recapture my youth, our 1965 Mustang is my choice.

So what does all this have to do with selecting a computer? Simply put, it all comes down to what you want to use your computer for. If you have an old computer with a 386 processor sitting in the corner of your office and you wish to use it, then by all means dust it off, warm up your dial-up connection, and wait. Be sure to have plenty of coffee and magazines to read (and perhaps a little *NoDoz* would help too!).

Seriously, since you will want access to the Internet for online genealogy, you will need a computer fast enough to navigate safely and successfully on today's Information Super Highway – the Internet. As you wouldn't take a Vespa on a highway with a 75-mph speed limit, I am afraid your old computers just aren't going to make it. You'll need to upgrade.

So what's the best computer for doing genealogy? Something that can cope with the intense speeds on the Internet. You'll want plenty of storage capacity – as you are searching, you may want to copy pictures and/or videos – and they take a lot of space. Will you want to back things up on a CD? Build a genealogy blog to share research on your family names? As with selecting a car, a lot will depend on what you want to do with the computer.

Having admitted earlier that I do not have a lot of technical aptitude, you may be wondering how I can possibly credibly suggest the type of computer for you to use. The answer is simple – I turned to several people far more expert than I on the topic, and asked their opinion in several key areas. It's interesting – I asked four computer experts and got four different answers (go figure!). However, I think you'll find their expertise helpful as you begin searching for a computer. Below are the recommendations from these four experts.

I asked each of them to provide their thoughts on the features of whatever computer an individual should purchase to do online genealogy. I asked for their input in these areas:

1. What processor should I look for?
2. Does the operating system matter, and if so, what is your recommendation?
3. How much RAM is required?
4. How much storage space is needed?
5. Etc. (Other thoughts)

Following are their recommendations:

Raymond T.

1. What processor should I look for? *Intel Core i3, Intel or AMD.*
2. Does the operating system matter, and if so, what is your recommendation? *Even though Microsoft is no longer supporting XP, it can still be used, but most likely at least Windows 7.*
3. How much RAM is required? *Depends on the Operating System: XP=2 GB minimum, Vista=3 GB minimum, Windows 7 = 3 GB or MUCH BETTER 4+GB*

4. How much storage space is needed? *250 GB except for Windows 7. Then, it is 325 GB or better.*
5. Etc. (Other thoughts) In addition to being incredibly technically adept, Raymond is a dynamic, prolific and extremely skilled genealogist. He strongly suggests using a laptop for doing genealogy, given its power abilities and portability. With a laptop, however, he had a warning: "*It should have at least a 15" screen (small screens won't support most of the data displays used in genealogy programs).* Other things Raymond suggested as necessary:

— *Wireless Internet capability*
— *A laptop should have at least 325GB of storage*
— *Must have at least a CD writer, preferably a DVD writer*
— *High-quality genealogy software* (Note: we'll discuss this more in-depth later in the book.)

Mike B.

1. What processor should I look for? *A Pentium processor at minimum.*
2. Does the operating system matter, and if so, what is your recommendation? *Doesn't really matter.*
3. How much RAM is required? *Computers with 2 GB RAM should be able to handle genealogy needs.*
4. How much storage space is needed? *A 200 GB hard drive should handle everything. 200 GB+ hard drives are common place now, even terabyte drives.*
5. Etc. (Other thoughts) Mike opined that computers have come a long way in recent years, and most reputable computers on the market these days should be able to handle online research. Other things Mike suggested as necessary:

— *Must have a cable or DSL connection*
— *A DVD writer is necessary*
— *A recent version of Internet Explorer or its equivalent is required*

— *Apple is a big player in the home computer world too*

Tim T.

Tim used a slightly different format than Ray or Mike, and I liked it, so thought I would share it below.

1. What processor should I look for?

— *Good: Pentium 4, Athlon 64*

— *Better: Dual core Pentium, Core 2 Duo, Athlon 64 X2*

— *Best: Core 2 Quad, Core i3 or i5, Phenom X3 or X4*

— *Insane: Core i7 or Phenom X6*

— *You're kidding, right? Anything earlier, I recommend avoiding anything with a Celeron or Sempron class (i.e. single core) processor.*

2. Does the operating system matter. If so, what is your recommendation?

— *You should be fine with Windows XP, Vista or 7. Stay away from any earlier Windows operating system.*

3. How much RAM is required?

— *Good: 1 GB*

— *Better: 2 GB*

— *Best: 4 GB*

— *Insane: 4+ GB*

— *You're kidding, right? Less than 1 GB*

4. How much storage space is needed?

— *Good: 40 GB*

— *Better: 100 to 500 GB*

— *Best: 500+ GB*

— *Insane: 1 TB*

— *You're kidding, right? Anything less than 40 GB*

5. Etc. (Other thoughts):

— *I'm a big fan of higher resolution monitors because the higher the resolution, the more screen "real estate" you have, meaning that you can see more things on the same screen at the same time. A dual-monitor configuration would be ideal.*

6. Laptops:

— *Good: 3G service, 384 Kbps download speed*

— *Better: 3G service, 1-2 Mbps download speed*

— *Best: 4G or WiFi service, 10+ Mbps download speed*

— *You're kidding, right? Any dial-up service*

7. Internet connection speeds:

Internet connection speed is as much a consideration as what type computer to use. Here are my recommendations

— *Good: DSL / Cable, 1.5 Mbps*

— *Better: DSL / Cable, 6-7 Mbps*

— *Best: DSL / Cable, 1.5 Mbps10 Mbps*

— *You're kidding, right? Any dial-up service / 56 Kbps*

One last thought: For the budget-minded person, I think there are a lot of older Pentium 4/Windows XP class PCs that would be sufficient for basic research and running most genealogy software. Good solid used PCs from Dell (Optiplex series) can often be purchased for less than $150. Currently there are a number of these PCs being replaced in Corporate America so there is a good supply of them. They will not set any speed records but my observation is that they are very reliable.

And finally, lest we offend any of the Apple/Mac users out there, some insights from that camp:

Michael W.

1. What processor should I look for?

– *Any Mac made within the last few years should be fine. The processor isn't really a factor in modern Macs. If you have an older machine make sure any software you install is compatible with the computer.*

2. Does the operating system matter, and if so, what is your recommendation?

– *If you are just using the Internet, any version of Mac OS X released in the past few years should be fine. If you are using specific software that is installed on your computer make sure to check the software requirements.*

3. How much RAM is required?

– *All you need is the minimum required by the OS. Of course, more is always better in this department.*

4. How much storage space is needed?

– *Whatever came with the computer will work. Data backup is the most important issue. There are many backup options available today. Data backup can be divided into two main categories. 1) Data backed up in your home on external hard drives. This involves using a program such as Apple's built-in Time Machine to back up data to an external drive connected to your computer or to your home network. This works well but has the downside of being in the same location as your computer. Whatever happens or your computer can also happen to your backup (flood, fire, theft). 2) Internet based data back up. There are many companies that offer data backup to the "cloud." This can be slower but has the advantage of keeping a copy of your data safe in the event of theft, fire, flood or other disaster. My personal opinion? Use both for your important documents.*

5. Etc. (Other thoughts). With the extreme popularity of iPads and iPhones, many applications have been developed to aid people with genealogy. Some of these apps are stand alone apps and some of them are companion apps that interface with their web counterparts. *Ancestry.com* is a site that allows you to use the app to access your online

data. Read reviews for the apps that interest you to make sure they will work with the website that you like to use. If the app is in the iTunes App Store you can read the user reviews to see how others like and use the app.

Other Costs

When you are pricing desktop computers, make sure a monitor and operating system are included. Some systems include either a 15", 17" or 18" monitor in the price. I would suggest getting the largest monitor you can afford. The larger monitors are easier on your eyes as you scour old records and documents. As of this writing, 21" to 24" monitors cost about $125 to $175 more than the smaller monitors configured with the systems.

Note – I have had great luck purchasing monitors online through an online auction system for significant discounts over new monitors.

Remember that most prices for new computers include the operating system, but do not include the MS Office suite of software – Word, Excel, Power Point, etc. That will add $125 to $300 to your purchase, depending on what version and type you purchase. Add to that genealogy software (discussed later in this book), most of which is reasonably priced below $45.

Okay – so you have scoured the Internet looking for systems that match the above specifications. Now you'll probably ask: "What's the best brand of computer to buy?" To answer your question, I'll ask you another question: "What's the best brand of car to buy?" I think you'll find all the above brands of computers and others too will be more than adequate to meet your online genealogy needs. It all depends on the experience people have had using each of the computers, and which ones they're comfortable with. In my extended family, we have an HP, Dell, Toshiba, Gateway and Mac.

4. SEARCHING

As you venture into the Internet world in search of your ancestors, several tools, resources, etc., will be of value to you. The first we'll cover is search engines, a key ingredient to your recipe for genealogical success.

Search Engines

Since you are focusing on doing genealogy online, you'll need to know a little about search engines – they are the vehicles you'll use to find all those genealogical treasures that are online. Search engines help you crawl through the bazillions (or is it trazillions?) of family history gems that can be found online. Good search engines also allow you to limit the number of hits you get for any search so that it is manageable (see the next section in this chapter labeled *Boolean Operators.*). If you type in *Daniel Quillen* and get 8,432,000 hits, that can be a little overwhelming. But knowing how to use search engines, and perhaps even which search engines to use, will help you home in on the information you are seeking much more rapidly, without having to wade through hundreds / thousands of hits that have nothing to do with what you are looking for. Following are a number of search engines you might consider using for your genealogical searches (note – all have .com appended to them: AOL.com, Ask.com, etc.):

Altavista
AOL
Ask
Bing

Google
Lycos
Yahoo

I find that each of these general-purpose search engines provides me with pretty much the same experience when searching for genealogical information. Some are a little more discriminating, others more inclusive. When I searched for my ancestor Leonidas Horney using the string "Leonidas Horney," I got the following number of hits through these various search engines:

Altavista – 38
AOL – 27
Ask – 21
Bing – 40
Clusty – 56
Google – 293
Lycos – 37
Yahoo – 37

There are a couple of tools on the web that will help you learn more about search engines, what they are, how to get the most out of them, and tricks of the search engine trade. One of the better ones is *Best Search Engines* by Wendy Boswell (*www.websearch.about.com*). She has a good handle on each of the search engines, shares tips and tricks, and generally provides you with information that will be good to know as you begin using new search engines. I have also had success in finding up-to-date articles on using search engines by typing something like the following into whatever search engine I am using: "How to get the most from search engines."

As you work with the Internet to find genealogical information, you'll get better and better. If your search yields too many hits to viably check, add new or different key words to help narrow the search. One of my ancestors is Samuel McCollough of Bristoria, Pennsylvania. If I search for "Samuel McCollough" I will receive upwards of 1.7 million hits. But if I narrow the search by adding the key word *death* or *died*, the number of hits drops to 200 to 500 hits – much more manageable. I happen to know he died in the 1870s, so adding 1870 as a key word narrows the number of hits to under 100 – a much more manageable number to deal with than 1.7 million. I could also add key words such as Bristoria and/or Pennsylvania, or his birth date, spouse's name, etc. The section that follows this on Boolean Operators gives you more hints and tips on how to get the most from your search engines and how to enter these key words in a manner that will yield the most accurate results.

Most of these search engines also have *Advanced Search* capabilities that will prompt you for more information that will make the search more discriminating and accurate. For example, after searching for Samuel McCollough and getting too many hits to work with on Google, I can narrow the search by locating the *Advanced Search* link at the bottom of the page and then clicking it. Once there, you can add search criteria that will aid your search.

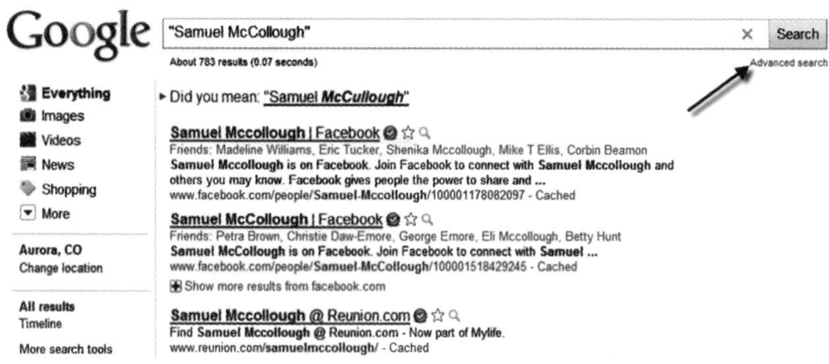

Metasearch engines are search engines that submit your request to a number of other search engines, databases, sites and web portals. The idea of metasearch engines is that no one search engine can possibly search all available information sources, so your request is launched through numerous search engines at the same time, and all the results are returned to you in one place. These are far more powerful search engines, but may yield you a TON or two of hits. But I have found them especially valuable when I have been searching for a needle in a haystack – those searches on general purpose engines that yield few or no hits. Some metasearch engines include *Dogpile.com, Mamma.com, Brainboost.com, Leapfish.com, Metacrawler.com,* etc. If this is an avenue you are interested in pursuing, simply type *metasearch engines* into your general purpose search engine and you'll receive plenty of information. Alternately, you can go to the Wikipedia site for search engines and they provide you a list of such engines: *en.wikipedia.org/wiki/List_of_search_engines*

I've mentioned Boolean Operators several times in this section; let's move on and learn about these bad boys.

Boolean Operators

Boolean Operators may seem like a name given by the local police department to a sinister group of nefarious perpetrators. But they are definitely not! They are in fact tools that will assist you greatly in narrowing the tremendous number of hits you may get for a particular ancestor. As I will do throughout this book, let me use one of my ancestors as an example of the power of these tools.

Leonidas Horney was a war hero from near the mid-western town of Rushville, Illinois. I have researched his life many times on the Internet, county libraries and at the Library of Congress. His surname, however, unfortunately will sometimes yield somewhat…embarrassing…results when I search without Boolean operators.

When I pull up Google (my favorite all-purpose search engine) and type in Horney, I get over 2.5 million hits.

If I include his entire name, I narrow the hits to 117,000! That's much better, although to be frank, I would be as likely to check every one of 117,000 hits as I would be of checking 2.65 million hits! But many of the initial hits are specific to this third great grandfather of mine. But after awhile, the hits become less…specific to him. If only there was a way to narrow the search further. 117,000 is still a lot of hits to review to glean information!

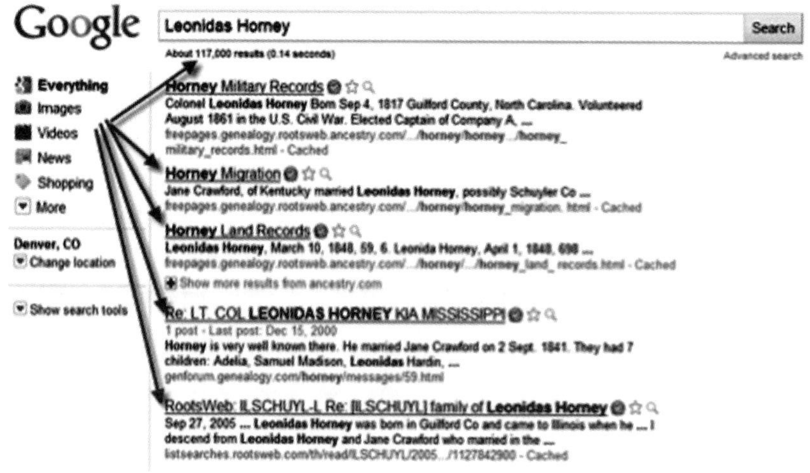

The first and simplest Boolean operators to use are the good old common household quotation marks: " ". Placing quotation marks around two or more words tells the Internet to search for them as though they are one term. Therefore, "Leonidas Horney" in quotes like this means the Internet should only return hits for Leonidas Horney (and not Leonidas Smith and Aaron Horney, for example).

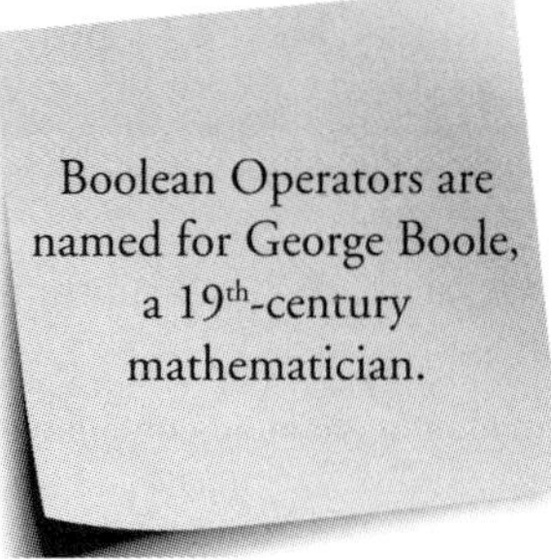

Boolean Operators are
named for George Boole,
a 19th-century
mathematician.

Much better! 348 is a much more manageable number than several of those earlier attempts. As I peruse many of the 348, I find many that have to do with his military career – which was long and distinguished – as well as many other items of interest. One hit, for example, takes me to a story that tells me that Leonidas, as the county surveyor, laid out the town of Littleton, Illinois. Numerous others provide the telephone numbers for individuals named Leonidas Horney.

Note – some search engines use the Boolean operator WITH instead of quotation marks: Leonidas with Horney should yield the same results as using quotation marks.

But – what if I am only interested in finding information about his marriage and wife? I can sift through those 348 records to see if I can find something that speaks of his marriage. Or – I can narrow the search further by using the quotation marks and the Boolean operator *AND*:

"Leonidas Horney" and "Married." This will search the Internet for *Leonidas Horney* as one search item (because of the quotation marks), and provide me only those hits that include Leonidas Horney *and* the word "Married." When I do that, I narrow the number to a more manageable 60 hits:

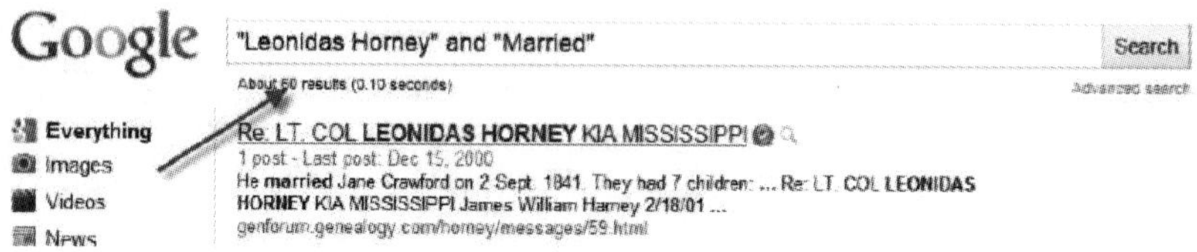

I learn quickly that Leonidas married Jane Crawford without having to weed through other locations that deal with his military exploits – as interesting as they are!

Another Boolean operator – not as strictly useful as some others, in my opinion – is *OR*. Most search engines default to the Boolean *OR* – they assume you want information either for one or the other words you type; that's why I get 117,000 hits when I enter Leonidas Horney. I get hits for Leonidas as well as Horney, whether they appear next to or even near each other.

NOT is another Boolean operator that is supported by some search engines, but not all. I would use this operator to eliminate certain terms from the search string. In the example I gave earlier about seeking information on Leonidas's marriage, I might have also approached it by typing in "Leonidas Horney" not "Civil War." That would yield more hits than "*Leonidas Horney" and married*, but fewer than might otherwise be received.

Remember – Boolean operators will help you in your Internet searches by making the numbers of hits you receive more manageable than they might otherwise be. If you get good at using Boolean operators, Bully for you! (Or, maybe: *Booly* for you!)

Family Surname Groups

Another helpful tool to find your ancestors are family surname groups. Through the years, many such groups have sprung up over the world – thousands, perhaps tens of thousands – are often available right at your fingertips.

Several years ago I stumbled across a family surname group and reaped huge rewards. As I was doing research on another book, I ran across a genealogy group doing research on the Hudson name. As indicated earlier, Hudson is my maternal grandmother's maiden name. I jotted down information about the group and later contacted them. I explained that I had run across their association and wanted to join. They responded immediately (most will) and asked for whatever genealogical information I could supply about my line of the Hudson family.

This was a line I hadn't done much research on, but I provided what I knew – information about me, my folks and grandparents, and the names of my great grandfather and great grandmother.

A few weeks later, I received a note welcoming me to the Hudson Family Association (HFA). Accompanying the welcome note was a copy of *The Hudsonian*, the association's quarterly publication. As I idly thumbed through it, I noted with delight that in the *Welcome New Members* section, my name was listed, along with the genealogy information I had provided. But that's not all. Someone in the association had tied me into research done by the HFA, and they provided genealogy information that picked up from my great grandfather, who was born in 1877, and took it back eleven generations from me – to 1541! What a delicious and welcome surprise. Included were the names of the husbands and wives of each generation, along with their birth dates and places. I fired off a missive seeing if they had anything like family group sheets for these families, and within a very short time I had the family group sheets for all seven generations beyond my great grandparents. Names, dates and sources for those names and dates were

THE LOST QUILLEN

A number of years ago I learned that descendants of the first McQuillan/Quillen to come to America hosted a family meeting and brunch for all McQuillan / Quillen descendants on the fourth Sunday of each August in Gate City, VA. The meeting and luncheon were held in an old Church that was built on land a long-gone Quillen had donated to the church, with the stipulation that the fourth Sunday of every August was reserved for the family to meet at and use the chapel and building.

We met inside the chapel, and during the opening remarks, each person attending was asked to stand and introduce himself or herself to the gathered family members. A part of the introduction was identifying which branch of the family you belonged to. When it came time for me to introduce myself, I did so, indicating that I wasn't exactly certain which branch of the family I belonged to, since my great grandfather and his family had left Virginia in the late 1800s.

After introductions, a member of the family from the area took it upon himself to introduce me to other members of the family. He delighted in introducing me as "the lost Quillen." On one occasion, he introduced me to a very distinguished elderly gentleman named Jimmy Quillen. As soon as he heard I was the "lost Quillen," he squinted up into my face thoughtfully, then said, "Lost, huh? That must mean you are a Democrat!" I later learned that Jimmy was *Senator* Jimmy Quillen, Republican senator for 34 years representing Tennessee! Lost Quillen indeed!

there for each of the families – a true treasure. And all because I had "accidentally" or perhaps coincidentally – come across information about that family.

So – what do you need to do to find family associations like that? Well, since we're talking about online genealogy, the first thing I would suggest is going to the Internet. Open your favorite search engine and type in *(Surname) genealogy* and see how many hits you get. You will most likely find message boards, forums, genealogy groups, books about your ancestors, etc. Using the Boolean operators we discussed earlier in this chapter should yield a manageable number of hits where you can start your perusal. Even surnames that are as common as Smith, Jones, Quillen, etc., will likely yield many hits. When I searched under Quillen Genealogy, I received over 141,000 hits; however, when I used one of the more obscure surnames in my family tree – Stunkard – I received 7,450 hits.

Funeral Home Records

I am embarrassed to say that for years (and years), I have skipped over funeral home records, first because I wasn't even aware of them, and second because I simply didn't think they would be of much use to me. Boy, was I wrong! I stumbled across this incredible resource while searching for information about my second great grandfather, Jonathan Baldwin Quillen, and once I found the value of these records, I vowed to always include them whenever appropriate for my family members.

And what makes them so valuable? First, many of them are available online (I often access them through USGenWeb.org). Second, they often provide information that other records don't provide, and third, they provide information that would have to be gleaned from other records. Take for example, the funeral home record of my second great aunt, my great grandfather's sister:

> **Henslee, Lizzie Lutitia**: Hartville, MO; died at Baptist Hospital on Jun 12, 1963; housewife; born Apr 3, 1877 in Nashville, TN; d/o J. B. Quillen and Sarah Burk; widow; 1 daughter Mrs. Wayde Carlisle of Stockton, MO; 2 sons Lester and Chester; 3 brothers Evan of Aberdeen, WA, Ed of Ralston, OK and Henry of Pawnee, OK; 3 grandchildren; 6 great-grandchildren. Burial at Steele Memorial Cemetery.

Let's consider the various bits of information available from this one online source:

— Corroboration of the spelling of her married name. In the county where she lived, there were families who spelled their name Hensley, and others who spelled it Henslee. I had seen her name spelled both ways, and this would appear to corroborate the latter spelling for her.
— her middle name (although the spelling varies from other sources I have);
— her residence at the time of her death;
— her death date;
— her birth date;
— her birth place;
— the names of her parents;
— her husband preceded her in death;
— the name and residence of her daughter's husband;
— the names of her two sons;
— the names and residences of three of her brothers;
— the cemetery in which she was buried.

Her funeral record provided a treasure trove of genealogical information. Much of it would be considered secondary information and not primary, but all of it is helpful in piecing together the picture of her life. While I previously had much of this information, had I not had it, this would have been a great boon to my research. As it was, it confirmed several items of information and provided some new information.

Bottom line – don't do as I did and pass over funeral home records when you run across them. Yes, they are secondary sources for most information, but they can also be a great assist in your research, providing a plethora of information that would require many other records to duplicate.

Genealogy Societies

Another rich source of online genealogical information can be found in genealogy societies. These societies, typically focusing on genealogical research in a particular geographic area (typically county or state), can be found in every state of the union, and most counties in those states typically have at least one such society. These societies are often formed with the specific purpose of hunting down, preserving and sharing genealogical documents – birth and death records, marriage records, Bible records, obituaries, etc., etc. They are often peopled by zealous volunteers who patiently and doggedly search for any and all records of genealogical value, then work to preserve them and make them available to anyone wishing to use them in their research.

Societies such as this are often responsible for recording the gravestones found in cemeteries, abstracting birth, death and marriage records, indexing censuses for the county – in short, about any area of genealogical research you can think of. And a plus for distant researchers – in recent years, these societies have worked hard to get as many of their records online as possible, as they recognize the immense value of making the records available to others.

One of the easiest ways to find the websites of genealogy societies is to Google them. Simply type the name of the area you are looking for, followed by genealogy society:

— *Hawkins County, Tennessee genealogy society*
— *Sullivan County, Tennessee genealogy society*
— *Pennsylvania genealogy society*
— *Tennessee genealogy society*

Online Death Certificates

Many states have begun putting their vial records online, including death certificates. Like funeral home records, these were records that I more or less overlooked for years, until I began to understand the value and volume of the information available through them. Considered a primary resource for death information (date, cause, location of burial), death certificates also often provide interesting and informative secondary information – birth dates and places, names of parents, including the mother's maiden name, and sometimes that names of children, spouse, etc.

Many states' death certificate sites are free, while others make those records available through Vitalrec.com. The cost for certificates through Vitalrec.com is governed by each individual state, but a typical cost is $10 to $15 per certificate.

Notwithstanding the fact that some states make their vital records available through subscription sites (or sites that charge for each certificate), a number of states also provide the information free of charge – if you use a little persistence to find them! Missouri is one of those states. I was searching for information on my great grandfather's death in Missouri, when I came across this death certificate for a great grandson of his:

FEB 23 193? MISSOURI STATE BOARD OF HEALTH
BUREAU OF VITAL STATISTICS
CERTIFICATE OF DEATH

Do not use this space.

4368

N.B.—Every item of information should be carefully supplied. AGE should be stated EXACTLY. PHYSICIANS should state CAUSE OF DEATH in plain terms, so that it may be properly classified. Exact statement of OCCUPATION is very important.

1. PLACE OF DEATH
County Wright
Township Clark
City (No. St. Ward)
Registration District No. 1122
Primary Registration District No. 6226
File No.
Registered No.

2. FULL NAME Norman Quillen
(a) Residence, No. St. Ward. (Usual place of abode) (If nonresident, give city or town and State)
Length of residence in city or town where death occurred yrs. mos. ds. How long in U.S., if of foreign birth? yrs. mos. ds.

PERSONAL AND STATISTICAL PARTICULARS

3. SEX M
4. COLOR OR RACE W
5. SINGLE, MARRIED, WIDOWED, OR DIVORCED (write the word) S
5a. IF MARRIED, WIDOWED, OR DIVORCED HUSBAND OF (OR) WIFE OF
6. DATE OF BIRTH (MONTH, DAY, AND YEAR) Apr. 9, 1932
7. AGE Years 3 Months 9 Days 13 If LESS than 1 day, hrs. or min.
8. Trade, profession, or particular kind of work done, as spinner, sawyer, bookkeeper, etc. None
9. Industry or business in which work was done, as silk mill, saw mill, bank, etc.
10. Date deceased last worked at this occupation (month and year)
11. Total time (years) spent in this occupation
12. BIRTHPLACE (CITY OR TOWN) (STATE OR COUNTRY) Mo.
13. NAME (Father) Hugh Quillen
14. BIRTHPLACE (CITY OR TOWN) (STATE OR COUNTRY) Mo.
15. MAIDEN NAME (Mother) Vada Tharp
16. BIRTHPLACE (CITY OR TOWN) (STATE OR COUNTRY) Mo.
17. INFORMANT (ADDRESS) Emmett Quillen
18. BURIAL, CREMATION, OR REMOVAL PLACE Curtis Cemetery 1/24 1936
19. UNDERTAKER (ADDRESS) [illegible] Norwood Mo
20. FILED 1-23 1936 Roy A Burnett Registrar

MEDICAL CERTIFICATE OF DEATH

21. DATE OF DEATH (MONTH, DAY, AND YEAR) 1/22 1936
22. I HEREBY CERTIFY, That I attended deceased from 1/11 1936 to 1/22 1936
I last saw h[illegible] alive on 1/22 1936 Death is said to have occurred on the date stated above, at 11 P m.
The principal cause of death and related causes of importance were as follows: Date of onset
Pneumonia
Other contributory causes of importance: Flu
Name of operation Date of
What test confirmed diagnosis? Was there an autopsy?
23. If death was due to external causes (violence), fill in also the following:
Accident, suicide, or homicide? Date of injury 19
Where did injury occur? (Specify city or town, county, and State)
Specify whether injury occurred in industry, in home, or in public place.
Manner of injury
Nature of injury
24. Was disease or injury in any way related to occupation of deceased?
If so, specify
(Signed) R. J. Vannoy M. D.
(Address) Norwood Mo

Consider the information I was able to glean from this certificate that went beyond his date and place of death:

— his birth date;

— his precise age at death;

— where he was born;

— his residence at the time of his birth;

— his father's name and his mother's maiden name

— the name of the informant (from other records, I know this is his grandfather);

— his place of burial

— his date of burial

— the cause of death – pneumonia.

As you can see, online death certificates provide additional sources of information that while secondary, can lead to the discovery of primary resource records.

A special note about immigrants. Near the top of this form is an area for the person providing the information to indicate how long this individual had been in the United States if they were foreign born. This could be a key that helps unlock the mystery of when an immigrant ancestor came to America, and a key bit of information that will help find immigration records that can provide abundant amounts of genealogical information.

To find online death certificates, type the name of the area along with death certificates: *Missouri death certificates, Wright County, Missouri death certificates, New York death certificates*, etc.

Local Histories

During the early to late 1800s, it became a popular practice of communities (counties, towns, etc.) to commission the writing of community histories. Many of these histories are available on dusty bookshelves of county and town libraries. But thanks primarily to the efforts of local genealogy societies, many of these histories are being posted online. Consider for a moment the history for my fourth-great grandfather — Samuel Horney — which I found online one day while poking around for information on his son, Leonidas Horney. It was contained in the community biography called *Old Settlers of Schuyler County, Illinois* (author's note: I do *not* look like my fourth-great grandfather):

SAMUEL HORNEY

Honorable Samuel Horney was born in Guilford County, North Carolina, October 18th, 1788. His father, Phillip Horney, was born in Maryland about the year 1758; his vocation was that of a farmer. On the 12th of

March, 1782, he was married to Miss Sarah Manlove, the daughter of William Manlove, Esquire, of Maryland. Soon after his marriage he moved to Guilford County, North Carolina, and there engaged in agricultural pursuits. As the fruits of this union, they had a family of four sons, of which the subject of this sketch is the fourth. His wife died in the year 1795, and in 1801 Mr. Horney married Miss Anne Carter. They had a family of five children. The father died at his residence in North Carolina in the year 1821. His second wife survived him until May 6th, 1844. Samuel Horney received his early education in the schools of Guilford County, North Carolina. After leaving school he turned his attention to teaching, and previous to his marriage he held the positions of constable and deputy sheriff of his native county, and on the breaking out of the war of 1812, he enlisted, in 1813, in the army at Richmond, Virginia, for the duration of the war. He was placed in command of a rendezvous, and was recruiting sergeant until the next spring. He then marched the men to Fredericksburg, Virginia, and was there formed into a company, commanded by Captain John P. Duvall.... In 1815 he was mustered out, and returned to his home, and on the 11th of August, 1816, he was married to Miss Emilia Charles, daughter of Elijah Charles, Esquire. The fruit of this marriage was his only child, the late Colonel Leonides Horney, who was born near the old family homestead in

SAMUEL HORNEY.

North Carolina. After his marriage, Mr. Horney was engaged in teaching until July, 1818, when, with his family, he moved to St. Clair County, Illinois, which state was then a territory. In the spring of 1825 he removed to Schuyler County, and settled near Rushville, where he resided until 1832. In the Black Hawk war he served as quartermaster of the 4th Illinois regiment. The division was commanded by General Whitesides. Soon after the war he purchased the farm near Littleton, on which he now resides.

Mr. Horney was one of the first three commissioners who assisted in the organization of Schuyler County, and hence he is properly classed among the old settlers. In 1836 he was elected Justice of the Peace, and held that office, by re-election, until 1866. In 1843 he served in the legislature as representative from Schuyler County. Mr. Horney and wife are both residing at their residence, hale and hearty, considering their advanced age. Mr. Horney is a man who is highly beloved and respected by his fellow citizens, and the people speak of him with a just pride, as being one of the honored fathers of the county. He is among the few who are surviving who figured in the first organization of the county. Politically, he says he is a supporter of the old Jeffersonian principles.

Consider the incredible amount of information available in this short life sketch of this hero of Schuyler County, Illinois, reaching back over 250 years:

— he was considered honorable (can't exactly say that about *all* my ancestors!)
— his birth date and place
— the fact that his parents had four boys, and he was the youngest of that four
— a tremendous amount of information about his parents (my *fifth* great grandparents!), and even his mother's father – my sixth great grandfather

— information about his military career, which included the War of 1812 and the Blackhawk War (both of which contain records that may shed additional light on his life and family)
— the fact that he had only one son, my third great grandfather, and his birth place
— his grandparents' marriage date and place
— his various vocations (farmer, teacher, deputy, constable, etc.)
— his movement through the years (especially important if other children had been born during the moving years)

Again, it is important to remember that this is all secondary data, but can be used to guide me to primary sources of information. Some of those sources, due to the age of this gentleman, may never be found, so this information is critical indeed.

You may have to be creative to find these old histories online. You can find some of them by going to your search engine and typing in the name of a state or county, followed by the word *history* or *genealogy*. You may have to play around a little with search words, but the effort may yield great results for you.

Don't forget to look for local histories!

Message Boards

Through the years I have been fortunate enough to glean a great deal of genealogy from other genealogists – genealogists (generally speaking) are more than happy to share their research with others, primarily because they have most likely been the recipient of information from other genealogists in the past. One of the best ways to "meet" those who are doing genealogy on the same lines as you are is through **genealogy message boards**. These message boards are generally associated with free and subscription genealogy services such as Cyndi's List, Genealogy.com, Ancestry.com, Rootsweb, etc. They are easy to find: you can either type in the words *Genealogy message boards* into your search engine, or you can simply type the surname for which you are searching along with the word genealogy: *Quillen genealogy*, for example. Doing so will yield a host of websites, and almost always one or more will be a message board. Here are some samples from when I typed in *Quillen genealogy*:

Each of these websites leads me to a different message board with information about Quillen genealogy. I can of course narrow the search by adding more qualifying information: Quillen Genealogy Lee County, VA, for example. By clicking on one of these many links, I'll find something like this:

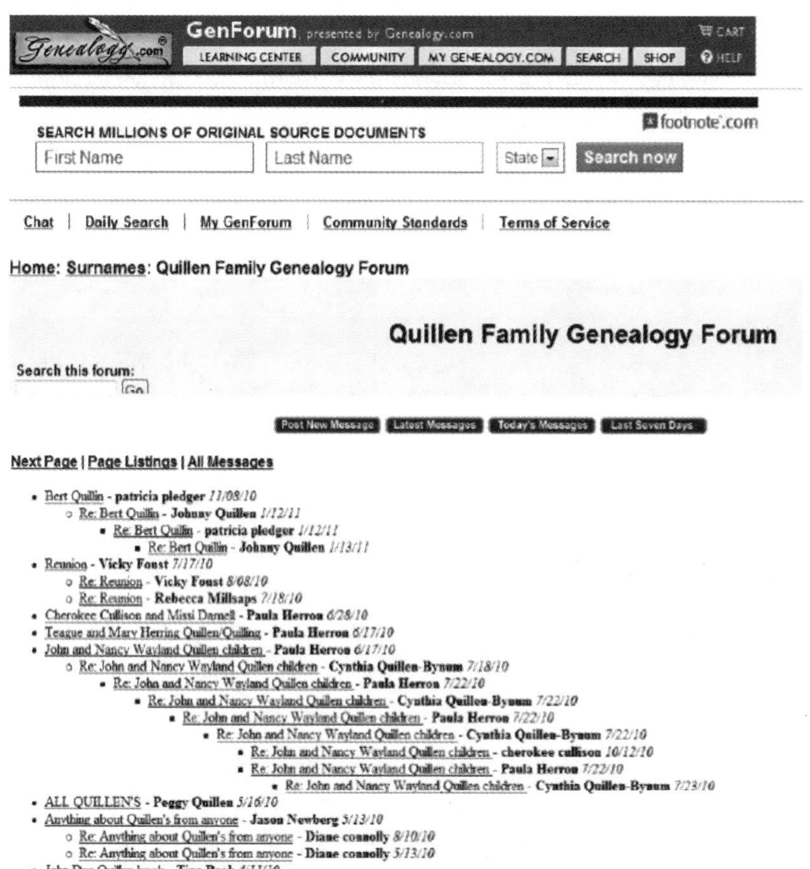

Each of these links is a question or answer – communication – about Quillen genealogy. You'll note that this is a very active message board – check the dates of the messages – nearly two dozen entries in an eight month period. Sometimes (often), you'll note that requests for information were posted many years ago. In early 2010 I ran across a message that had been posted on a message board in 2004 by someone looking for information on Thomas McCollough and Sarah Dunn. I discovered it while doing research on my McCollough line. Hoping the requestor hadn't changed her e-mail address since 2004, I fired off an e-mail to her. Within hours she responded and I have developed a great friendship with this distant McCollough cousin whose passion is also genealogy. (Interesting side note – this cousin – Aurianna – is an avid genealogist as well as paranormal – I suppose the two hobbies are related!). Since our e-mail meeting, we have exchanged significant amounts of genealogy, photographs and stories of our ancestors.

Old Newspapers

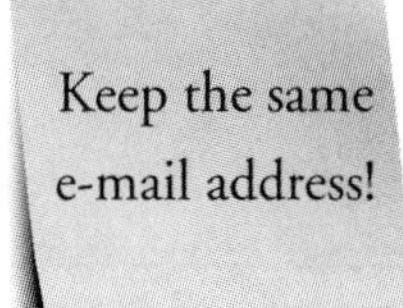
Keep the same
e-mail address!

Often overlooked resources for genealogical information are local newspapers of the last two-ish centuries. What? Your ancestor wasn't rich or famous, didn't commit any crimes (that you know of!), etc., so they surely wouldn't be newsworthy? Don't be so fast to decide that is the case. Especially in the 1800s and well into the 1900s (even today in some small communities), special events such as births, deaths and marriages found their way into the pages of the local newspapers. Even beyond that, small town newspapers and county newspapers were always looking for information that was newsworthy and of interest to their readership. A daughter who had married and moved away, but was visiting to help her sister after the birth of a child may well have made the society pages of the local newspaper.

Following are a sampling of the types of genealogical information you can find in old newspapers:

Context

Okay, so perhaps context isn't exactly a genealogical treat, but I love to use the newspapers to get a feel for the life my ancestors led, in the communities where they led them. Advertisements from local shops and vendors gave me an idea of the price of things. Classified ads helped me learn what the cost of a home was during that era, as well as rent, the cost of a horse or cow, etc. I think it adds color and life to my ancestors.

School Day Specials for Saturday

GINGHAM DRESSES

$1.48 values at 98c $1.98 values at $1.69
$2.98 values at $2.45 $3.98 values at $3.35
$4.95 values at $3.95 $5.95 values at $4.95

SCHOOL MIDDIES

$2.25 values at $1.89 $2.98 values at $2.69
$3.98 values at $3.45 $4.95 values at $4.35

The better grades at reduced prices.

Ribbons—special lot at..........................39c yard
Black Ribbed Hosiery, all sizes 39c
(Three pairs, $1.00)

Birth Announcements

Life events such as births, deaths and marriages were big deals and were especially of interest to small town citizens and were usually carried in the local newspaper. At a minimum, birth announcements generally provide information about the parents, at least, and often grandparents. I have even seen them provide information about brothers and sisters, although that is generally the exception and not the rule (too bad!).

BIRTH ANNOUNCEMENT

Dr. and Mrs. R. W. Corbett announce the birth of a fine nine-pound baby girl, born at their home at 321 Adams street at 1 a. m. today, who has been named Elsie Jane. Both mother and babe are doing nicely.

Friends of Dr. Corbett tell a story on him to the effect that early this morning, before the child had attained the age of twelve hours, he went to a neighbor's chicken roost and borrowed one of the inmates, taking it over to show to the child. "Doc" must have a very intelligent offspring.

Obituaries

At the other end of the spectrum of life from birth announcements are obituaries. Obituaries can also be sources of genealogical information that might otherwise be elusive. Consider the obituary for my second great grandmother, Sarah Minerva Burke Quillen, from the local newspaper in her home town. Dated September 29, 1932, it read:

> Sara Burke Quillen was born October 3, 1843 in Lee County, Virginia, and died September 27, 1932, aged 89 years, 11 months and 24 days. She professed faith in Christ at an early age. When she was 20 years old, she married J.B. Quillen and to this union were born 9 children. She was preceded in death by her husband; a son; a daughter. Survivors are 6 sons, E. V. of Norwood, T. F., Henry and Ed Quillen, all of Ralston, OK, Evan Quillen of Aberdeen, WA and Creed Quillen of Mitchell SD; a daughter, Mrs. Henslee of Hartville.

A couple of genealogical gems are available through his obituary:

- Her birth date as calculated from her death date. Often, the birth date isn't listed as it is here; this obituary saved me having to do the math (I did it anyway!). The month and day of her birth agree with other records I have, but not the year. Other records I have show her birth date as 1845, not 1843.
- We know where she was living when she died (Hartville, MO).
- We learn that her husband, a son and daughter died before she did.
- She had seven living children at the time of her death.
- The married name of one of her daughters

Many of the obituaries I have reviewed through the years, especially those covering rural areas, will say something like: "JB Quillen died last Friday...." While I may have the date of the newspaper, that doesn't help me determine what *date — relative to the date of the newspaper* — he died on. If that is the case for one of your ancestors, there are a number of day-of-the-month calculators on the Internet. One I have found intuitive and easy to use is: *www.searchforancestors.com/utility/dayofweek.html.* Check it out and then bookmark it.

You can use it to determine what date a person died on if the obituary simply identifies a day of the week. Let me give you an example. This is the opening sentence of the obituary for my 2nd great aunt, Lizzie Leticia Quillen Henslee, Sarah's daughter:

> Lizzie Henslee, 86, daughter of J.B. and Sarah Minerva Quillen, was born April 3, 1887 near Nashville, TN and died Wednesday.

Her obituary appeared in the newspaper on June 20, 1963. As you can see, it is important for me to learn what date Wednesday was relative to the date the obituary was published, so I can pinpoint exactly the date of her death. If you go to the website I provided above and input the date as directed, it tells you that June 20, 1963 was a Thursday, so the Wednesday before that was June 19, 1963. Simple, right? Yes, except be careful…even this little bit of detective work can lead you to a wrong conclusion. I was fortunate to find Lizzie's death certificate, and it lists her death date as Wednesday, June 12, 1963 – not June 19. Everything you read in the newspapers isn't exactly perfect!

Miss Frances Peterson went to Fayette this morning and will teach in the high school there.

Mr. and Mrs. Fred Black and Miss Sue Judt motored to Fulton yesterday and spent the day with the latter's relatives.

Mrs. B. F. Seymour returned home last light from a visit with friends in Decatur, Ill.

W. T. Van Cleve returned this morning from Kansas City where he attended the wedding of his brother, J. K. Van Cleve, Saturday morning.

Miss Sarah Taylor left this morning for Lexington, Mo., to resume her studies at Central College.

Henry Green left today to enter Westminster College at Fulton.

Walter Burke returned to Columbia last night after spending the week-end here with his mother, Mrs M. W. Burke.

There are a number of online sources for obituaries: Legacy.com (*www.legacy.com/NS/explore/*) is one I have used extensively for deaths that have occurred in the previous 85 years or so.

Wedding Announcements

These are always fun and informative little news blurbs to run across. First of all – wedding announcements (generally) meant happy times for your ancestors. Secondly, I cannot recall an engagement or wedding announcement from a newspaper that *didn't* include the maiden name of the bride and the names of the bride's and groom's parents! The late 19th and early 20th centuries are the timeframes when these announcements became fairly standard in American newspapers, regardless of the social stature of the couple.

Society Pages

In small towns, births and deaths, weddings and visits from distant family members were important news, and society pages often yield information that will lead to further discoveries. In many newspapers I have reviewed, there are often several columns of bite-size information tidbits about this relative that was visiting from such-and-such a city.

A recent society page I reviewed provided snippets of what might be considered non-genealogical news, including Miss Peterson's return to Fayette to teach school. However, among seven entries on the society page I was reviewing from the Moberly Monitor Index from Moberly, Missouri on September 11, 1922, we learn that W.T. Van Cleve just returned from attending his brother's wedding, and that Walter Burke's mother is Mrs. M.W. Burke.

I had a friend who discovered one of her ancestors had a sister that my friend hadn't known about, because of an entry in the society page of the local newspaper that went something like:

> Ada and Phil Anderson celebrated their 15th wedding anniversary last Saturday at the city park. Among invited guests, her sister's daughter, Miss Anna Smithson from Toledo, was in attendance.

My friend had no idea that her ancestor Ada had a sister (much less a niece!) until she ran across this rather obscure society page article. Not only did she learn the sister's married name (Smithson) but she also learned her niece was living in Toledo.

Finding Old Newspapers

To find copies of old newspapers, understand that online access to newspapers is somewhat scanty, although several subscription and free services have sprung up in recent years that are adding to their collections all the time. But compared to other records (censuses, for example), the vast majority of newspapers that have been published in the US are not online. Companies that offer online access to newspapers are listed below.

Newspaper Archive

Newspaper Archive (*www.newspaperarchive.com*) is one of my favorite subscription services for looking up articles, obituaries, wedding announcements, etc., in old newspapers. Perhaps it's my favorite because it is one of the first such services I used for online genealogical research. I find it easy to use and intuitive to navigate. They boast they are the largest online newspaper archives out there, claiming they have "tens of millions" of full newspaper pages, adding one newspaper page *every second of the year* — about twenty-five million pages each year (that's a lot of work!). I like the service because it has good search capabilities, including a user-friendly advanced search, and covers many small town and county newspapers, not just the large city newspapers (most of my relatives seemed to favor rural life over big city life!). Their collection extends back to the mid-18th century through much more modern times. Subscription rates as of this writing are $6.00 per month for an annual subscription (translated: $72 for an annual subscription), or $10.00 per month for a monthly subscription. You can peruse their collection for free, but they limit you to about a half dozen pages per day; after that, you are provided with an opportunity to subscribe as a premium user. But before you subscribe, you can scan the newspapers they have in their collection, as well as the dates of the newspapers they have. An excellent service, in my opinion.

ProQuest Historical Newspapers

ProQuest is a collection available through your local library and possibly your local university library – individual subscriptions are not available. A number of libraries offer remote access to this service to their library patrons. ProQuest earned their reputation as an excellent source of historical newspapers beginning in 2001, when they began digitizing some of the major US newspapers – *Atlanta Constitution, Boston Globe, Chicago Tribune, Los Angeles Times, New York Times, Wall Street Journal, Washington Post,* etc. I have found this service effective for learning national and international headline news; but for my personal genealogical research, as mentioned above, most of my kin were in Backwater USA, so their information doesn't usually hit the big newspapers.

Ancestry.com

Ancestry.com has also gotten into the newspaper business also, which is a nice perq for those of us who have an Ancestry.com subscription. To reach their *Newspapers & Periodicals* section (currently consisting of over 1000 newspapers and 64 periodicals), from the *Home* page, select *Search*, then in the drop-down box, select *Card Catalog*. From there, enter *Newspapers &*

Periodicals in the *Keyword(s)* box, and voila! – you'll be whisked to their newspapers collection.

Their collection is much smaller than Newspaperarchive.com, with only 16 million pages (*only*!), from over 1,000 US, UK and Canadian newspapers, but it is growing all the time. Like Newspaperarchive.com, many of the newspapers are for small towns and counties, not just the big cities. Remember — you cannot subscribe to only the newspapers section of Ancestry.com — you get it as part of your membership to Ancestry.com. Subscription information about Ancestry.com is listed in the *Subscription Services* chapter.

Fold3

Footnote.com used to be one of my favorite websites. In late 2010 they were purchased by Ancestry.com, and their name was changed to Fold3. Their main focus has now become military records. They also have a good newspaper collection; it is located at *www.fold3.com/page/2539_newspapers_at_footnote.* Like ProQuest, Fold3's newspaper collection consists of the major historical newspapers in the US; unlike Proquest, Fold3 has partnered with SmallTownNewspapers (*www.smalltownnewspapers.com*) to reach into rural America, which I like and need for my personal research. Still, with only 250 to 300 small-town newspapers in their collection, it's pretty small potatoes compared to someone like NewspaperArchive.com. Subscription information is listed in the Subscription Services chapter.

GenealogyBank.com

GenealogyBank.com boasts a collection of newspaper articles from the late 1600s through the present day. They have articles, obituaries, etc., from approximately 4,500 newspapers. They have both historical newspapers as well as many rural ones. Once on their website, you can search by state to see their collection, thereby determining if a subscription is something you're interested in. As of this writing, you can have a thirty-day free trial; after that, subscriptions run $5.83 per month for an annual subscription ($69.96 annually) or $19.95 for a monthly subscription. A two-year subscription is even available, at $139.90 for the subscription.

SmallTownPapers.com

Mentioned above in the Fold3 section, SmallTownPapers focuses primarily on small-town newspapers, as their name suggests. Their website (*www.smalltownpapers.com*), like that of several others noted above, allows you to search through their titles to see if the newspapers or areas of the country you're most interested in are included in their collection. Their collection begins in 1865, and runs through current day. One nice thing about this service, although not nearly as extensive as some of the others listed here, is that there is no fee to access their collection.

Government Efforts to Preserve Old Newspapers

In addition to the various subscription services mentioned above, the federal government has gotten into the newspaper preservation act, and we can all benefit. There are several national projects focused on preserving the heritage of our country through its newspapers. Genealogy societies have been doing this for years, but in recent years the federal government has started several programs aimed at preserving our past. The National Endowment for the Humanities (NEH) partnered with the the National Digital Newspaper Program (NDNP) and the Library of Congress (LC) to work with every American state and many countries to provide enhanced access to United States and foreign newspapers published between 1836 and 1922. The NEH provides awards that support state projects to select and digitize *historically significant* titles that are aggregated and permanently maintained by the Library of Congress.

Note that the NEH isn't trying to digitize every United States newspaper between 1836 and 1922 – they are selecting *historically significant* newspapers. I haven't been able to find out what qualifies newspapers as historically significant. When I scan their titles, however, there is high representation among the major cities in each state where the projects are running. There is a program called *Chronicling America: Historic American Newspapers*, which, according to their website, is:

> ...a prototype of the digital resource being produced through NDNP, is freely available to Internet users everywhere. Users may search the digitized pages contributed by funded state projects and the Library of Congress as well as consult a national newspaper directory of bibliographic and holdings information to identify newspaper titles available in all types of formats. The directory was compiled through an earlier NEH initiative, the United States Newspaper Program.

Right now, the project is operating in 23 states and the District of Columbia. The states that are under way are Arizona, California, Florida, Hawaii, Illinois, Kansas, Kentucky, Louisiana, Minnesota, Missouri, Nebraska, New York, Ohio, Oklahoma, Oregon, Pennsylvania, South Carolina, Texas, Utah, Virginia, and Washington. (Sorry if the states you are doing research in aren't there yet!) Agencies and societies applied for grants ("awards") to undertake the project within their respective state. Award winners include state universities, historical societies, and public libraries. The program started in 2004, and they expect to have over four million newspaper pages online and accessible to the public by the end of 2011. Over two million pages are currently available. To determine what newspaper holdings they have, go to *http://chroniclingamerica.loc.gov*. A box will allow you to hunt for newspapers in their collection by the name of the newspaper. If you're not sure of the newspaper, look initially under the name of the county or town you are most interested in. For example, I am doing research in Wright County, Missouri; by going to the Ws, I find the following newspapers listed for Wright County Missouri:

Wright County Democrat. (Clarion, Wright County, Iowa) 1884-1905
The Wright County eagle. (Delano, Minn.) 1872-1881
Wright County home-talk. (Hartville, Wright County, Mo.) 1877-1881
Wright County journal-press. (Buffalo, Wright County, Minn.) 1930-current
Wright County monitor. (Clarion, Wright County, Iowa) 1869-current
The Wright County progress. (Hartville, Wright County, Mo.) 1893-1911
Wright County register. (Liberty, Wright Co., Iowa) 1868-1868
The Wright County reporter. (Dows, Wright County, Iowa) 1927-1963
Wright County Republican. (Monticello, Wright County, Minn.) 1859-1861
Wright County Republican. (Clarion, Wright County, Iowa) 1882-1884
Wright County republican. (Hartville, Mo.) 1911-1957
Wright County Republican. (Hartville, Mo.) 188?-18??

Note that a number of the newspapers are for Wright Counties of other states. However, I can identify four newspapers in this list that were published in Hartville, Wright County, Missouri, and the dates they were published. Hartville is where my Quillen ancestors lived for a spell, so these newspapers are all of interest to me.

Just for grins, I looked to see if there were any newspapers published in Hartville that used the name of the town and not the county. I found a couple of newspapers that were published in Hartville, MO:

The Hartville democrat. (Hartville, Mo.) 1889-1929
The Hartville news. (Hartville, Ohio) 1930-current
The Hartville press. (Hartville, Wright County, Mo.) 1890-189?
The Hartville uplift. (Hartville, Laramie County, Wyo.) 1910-1913

Clicking on any of the links listed in this section takes me to an information sheet that tells me the dates that they have copies of the newspapers, the frequency (weekly, daily, monthly), and what libraries have microfilms of the newspaper. If a newspaper is microfilmed and not available on the Internet (yet), you can order it through the inter-library loan process. One feature I liked is that the page also lets you search for other newspapers that might have been published in that city, county and state – so if you can identify just one newspaper covering the area you want, you can find others.

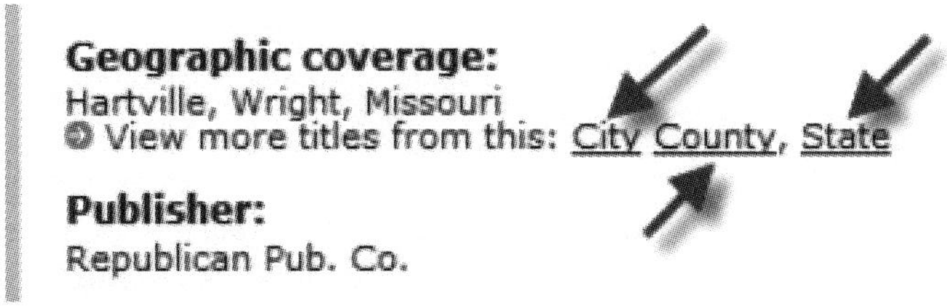

Geographic coverage:
Hartville, Wright, Missouri
View more titles from this: City County, State

Publisher:
Republican Pub. Co.

If you wish to search pages that are available online, (versus those that are available via inter-library loan on microfilm), you can go to *http://chroniclingamerica.loc.gov/search/pages/.* An **Advanced Search** page comes up that allows you to search for specific dates, or date ranges, one or more words, etc.

Chronicling America's plan is to digitize newspapers according to the following schedule:

- In 2007, 1900-1910
- In 2008, 1880-1910
- In 2009, 1880-1922
- In 2010, 1860-1922
- In 2011, 1836-1922

Once you locate the title of the newspaper for which you are searching, click on the title, and then you can click on "Libraries that Have It" near the top of the record for holdings (see *www.loc.gov/chroniclingamerica/*).

The forerunner to the *Chronicling America* program was the *United States Newspaper Program,* also funded by the *National Endowment for the Humanities.* Every state participated, and the NEH awarded funding for the preservation – microfilming – of America's newspapers. If you go to *www.neh.gov/projects/usnp.html#ENR,* you can see all the projects on a state-by-state basis.

For a time, I was a volunteer for Random Acts of Genealogical Kindness (*www.raogk.org*), and since I worked just a few blocks from both the Denver Public Library and the Colorado State Archives, I was able to go there on my lunch hours and look up microfilmed records of obituaries, birth and wedding announcements, etc. But with the USNP, many of the searches I conducted could have been accomplished by individuals requesting inter-library loan of the microfilmed newspapers from the state of Colorado.

Here is what the USNP's website says about their services:

> Microfilm copies of newspapers are generally available to researchers anywhere in the country through inter-library loan. Information from the states' and territories' projects is loaded into one national database, the Online Computer Library's World-Cat catalog available at *www.oclc.org/us/en/default.htm.*

The USNP website includes links to each state, where you'll find information about which newspapers (names and dates) have been microfilmed, which organization is leading the effort, and where you can find out more information about accessing those microfilmed copies. Most of the states participate in inter-library loaning for their microfilmed newspaper collections.

The Library of Congress and Inter-Library Loan

If you're unable to get to Washington DC to view these microfilms, never fear – they are available through inter-library loan to your state library, academic institution or to one of the fourteen regional national archives centers. You can go to the following link to see the Library of Congress's inter-library loan policy: *http://www.loc.gov/rr/loan/.* Books and microfilm can be borrowed for sixty days. Patrons must view them at the library to which they were loaned – you cannot take them home. Not every item in the Library of Congress catalog is actually held in the collection, and not everything in the collection can be lent or copied. Here is what the Library of Congress website says about their newspaper collection:

> The Library of Congress maintains one of the largest and most comprehensive newspaper collections in the world, comprised not only of the major papers published in all 50 states and territories of the United States, but also those published in most other countries of the world that have existed over the past three centuries. Almost all of the more than 500,000 reels of newspaper microfilm held by the Newspaper & Current Periodical, European, Asian, and African & Middle Eastern Divisions are available for inter-library loan. Only newspapers that have been microfilmed are available for loan.

In summary, if you are running into difficulties finding birth, death or marriage dates for an ancestor, consider checking out the local newspapers around the time the event in question occurred. You may find all the answers for which you are looking, or at least some significant clues that will assist you in your search.

Old Photographs

In addition to being incredibly interesting to look at (I always look at the men's *shoes*!), old photographs may provide you with information of genealogical interest. "Really," you ask? Read on.

When my grandmother passed away, my parents went to Oklahoma to help my grandfather pack up his home so he could move in with my folks in Colorado. My grandparents had purchased their home in 1928. At the back of their yard was a very small garage; it hadn't been used for cars for decades – storage was its main purpose in life. As my folks began emptying out the garage, they found a box with literally hundreds of pictures packed in it. The pictures had the names of all the individuals in the picture, and was almost always accompanied by a date.

I was very excited about this find, and shared my excitement with a brilliant co-worker of mine. He expressed interest in the pictures, and asked me to bring them in to work so he could see them. I was happy to oblige.

Once I brought the pictures in, he studied them closely. Two pictures in particular drew his interest. They had been taken of the same family, but it was obvious from the ages of the children that they had been taken a number of years apart. My friend turned to me and said, "This picture must have been taken in the early 1890s." I asked how he knew that, and he said, "Well, the teenage and adult women are all wearing wasp-waisted dresses. Those were all the fashion near the end of the Victorian era – from about 1887 to 1894." I took the picture from him and turned it over, and was flabbergasted to see the date written on the back was 1892.

But my friend wasn't finished tutoring me on fashions. Taking the later picture of the family, he said, "And this one was taken about ten years later." I asked, "Aside from the obvious aging of the children, how do you know that?" He pointed to my second-great grandfather sitting in the center of the picture. He was wearing a suit coat and a vest. Said my friend, "Look at this old gentleman. Note that the bottom button of his vest is unbuttoned. That's because King Edward was fat, and was uncomfortable with his vest buttoned all the way to the bottom. So he started leaving the bottom button of his vest unbuttoned, setting a fashion trend at the same time!" He went on to draw my attention to the waists of the women's dresses and indicated that they were much modified from their earlier waspishness – they were not quite so severe! Turning over the picture, I found the date – 1904! Amazing.

Many books and articles have been written on this topic by people far brighter than I. See, for example, *Dating Old Photographs, 1840 – 1929,* Family Chronicle / Moorshead Magazines Ltd, 2000 or *Dressed for the Photographer: Ordinary Americans and Fashion, 1840-1900,* Kent State University Press; 2nd edition (March 1997) It's a topic that has always fascinated me.

Don't forget to use old family photos!

Suffice it to say that clothing may be an assist to you as you try to determine the years that pictures of your ancestors were taken. I've a friend, a fellow genealogist, who has had some luck identifying some of his ancestors by the insignia on their Civil War-era uniforms.

If you are like me and have no fashion sense (old *or* new!), then there are other ways you can date photographs, at least to get an idea of when the photo was taken. If you understand the history and technology of photography, you may get a clue as to the age of the photos you're viewing. Below are some of the more common types of photographs.

Ambrotypes – Ambrotypes were popular during the Civil War period, from about 1860 to 1866. The photo was on a thin piece of glass and often had a thick black paper backing.

Cabinet Cards – These photographic images were popular from the early 1860s through the 1920s. Photographic images were printed on thin paper, which was then glued on cardboard stock (about two or three thicknesses of a modern-day postcard) that was about 4"x6". Sometimes cabinet cards from the 1870s and 1880s have a green tint to them, owing to the chemicals used to produce the photographs. It was also very common for the photographer to print the name of his business and the city of his studio on the front of the card – helping you place your ancestors in a geographic location, at least for that picture. On the previous page are cabinet cards of a third-great aunt and her son, and my third-great grandmother, Jane Crawford Horney.

Cartes de visite – Produced between 1860 and 1891, small photographs were affixed to cards. Often those cards were bound together into small photo albums. I have several of these featuring some Civil War era ancestors of mine. The images are about 2"x3 1/2", on card stock a little larger.

During their heyday, these little albums were called cardomania, and were incredibly popular.

Daguerreotypes – Daguerreotyping (photo below) was a photographic method developed by Frenchman Louis Daguerre. They were on the photographic scene from 1839 through about 1860, and required long exposure times. The key to identifying a Daguerreotype photo is to tilt it back and forth. The image will appear to change from a normal picture to a negative.

Tintypes – Tintypes were photo images placed directly on thin sheets of iron that had been painted or enameled black. These were very popular from the late 1850s through 1910. Photographs could be developed rapidly, so were a favorite of traveling photographers, who set up shop temporarily in towns as well as town, county and state fairs, etc.

I am told that some individuals can use hair styles to identify the approximate date of photographs. Also, the way the individuals in the photo were posed was often a clue to the date the photo was taken. From the late 1800s to the early 1900s, it was fashionable for photos featuring couples to have the man seated and the woman standing next to him, often with a hand or forearm on his shoulder.

Oft times, old family photos can be valuable for learning more about your family. Earlier in this chapter I mentioned that my parents found a box of old family photos that had been squirreled away for six or seven decades. In addition to being fascinating to look at, thanks to my wonderful great grandmother Emma Adelia Sellers, the backs of each of the photos was as valuable as the front, at least from a genealogical perspective. She had taken the time to write on the backs of each photo, including the names of each person in the photo, the date — at least the year – that each photo was taken, and often the place the photo was taken. I was then able to take that information and compare it to the genealogical information she had written in the center section of the family Bible and get to know these family members much better.

What? You don't have any old family photos? Don't dismay – start looking. Recently, I made contact with a cousin that was a little younger than my parents. He was from Kansas, but had a daughter that lives about twenty minutes from me in Denver. We arranged to meet when he was in town. When we got together, I was thrilled to see that he had brought a family photo album, with many photos of the family. I had some of the photos he had, but he also had many I had not seen. He had pictures of my grandparents (his uncle and aunt) as well as my great grandparents (his grandparents). Many of the photos he had were photos I had not seen. In particular, I was interested in a photo he had of a great aunt and uncle of mine that I was especially close to. This great aunt didn't like having her picture taken and avoided cameras like the plague. Yet he had several pictures of this woman who was precious to me. He readily agreed to scan many of the photos and send them to me via e-mail.

If you don't have photos, reach out to other members of the family – parents, grandparents, siblings, aunts, uncles and cousins. Some people couldn't care a fig for keeping pictures, but it seems there's always at least one person in each family that values and will keep and preserve photos. Once you find that person, today's technology makes sharing photos relatively simple.

If none of those direct family members have old family pictures, then expand your search. Hit the genealogy message boards (see the section on *Message Boards* earlier in this chapter), and instead of seeking genealogical information, ask about photographs. You may be pleasantly surprised at the responses – and photos – you'll get. A year or so ago I made contact with a distant cousin on my McCollough line through a message board. I think my second-great grandfather had a terrific mustache, and shared his picture with this cousin. Once I had shared his picture, my cousin Aurianna shared a picture of her uncles. Note the family resemblance, at least mustache-wise! My second-great grandfather is on the left, her uncles are on the right, next page:

Why didn't those mustache genes get passed down to me!?

Social Security Death Index

Another source of online information can be found through the federal government's Social Security Death Index (SSDI), which can be found at FamilySearch.org, Ancestry.com, and a host of other places that any good search engine can take you to.

The SSDI is a listing of all those who have passed away, who once registered for a Social Security card in the United States. The information is somewhat scanty, but again, provides genealogical clues for those who make the effort to look up the information. Take for instance the SSDI information for my grandmother, Alma Lowrance, as displayed on FamilySearch.org:

U.S. Social Security Death Index

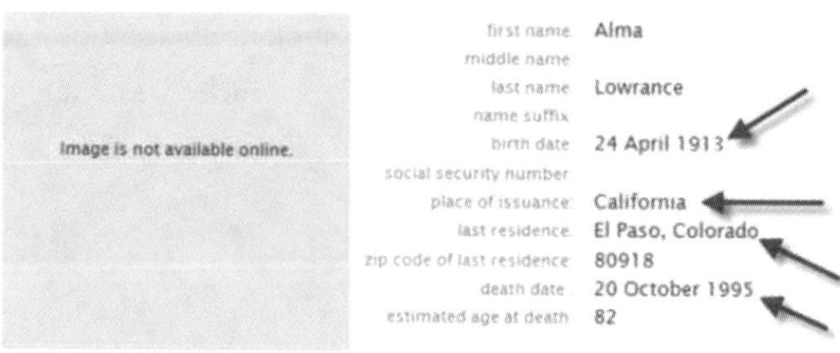

Image is not available online.

first name: Alma
middle name:
last name: Lowrance
name suffix:
birth date: 24 April 1913
social security number:
place of issuance: California
last residence: El Paso, Colorado
zip code of last residence: 80918
death date: 20 October 1995
estimated age at death: 82

From this record, I discover my grandmother's birth date, her social security number (I blanked it out) where she was living when she died, and her death date. I also learn where my grandmother's social security number was issued – California. If I hadn't already known, that is a clue as to where I might find the birth places of her children, perhaps a place of marriage, other family members, etc.

Dead-end Websites

(No – the title of this section isn't a pun; although it *would* be a good one...)

Every now and again, you are likely to find a link to a website you will be very excited about. With great anticipation, you click on the website, only to be confronted with this rather rude pronouncement:

The page cannot be found

The page you are looking for might have been removed, had its name changed, or is temporarily unavailable.

Please try the following:

- Make sure that the Web site address displayed in the address bar of your browser is spelled and formatted correctly.
- If you reached this page by clicking a link, contact the Web site administrator to alert them that the link is incorrectly formatted.
- Click the Back button to try another link.

HTTP Error 404 - File or directory not found.
Internet Information Services (IIS)

Technical Information (for support personnel)

- Go to Microsoft Product Support Services and perform a title search for the words **HTTP** and **404**.
- Open **IIS Help**, which is accessible in IIS Manager (inetmgr), and search for topics titled **Web Site Setup**, **Common Administrative Tasks**, and **About Custom Error Messages**.

Websites come and go, links are changed, and sometimes they are taken down or expire. When that happens, don't give up. There are several things you can do. First of all, look at the link you used. The link I had sought for in this example was *http://iltrails.org/schuyler/oldsettlersbio1.html#47.* The first thing you should try is erasing the last portions of the URL address. As you do so, you may find that the link was just broken at the end; going higher up on the URL address may bring you to a main page, where you can then access via a link the information for which you are looking.

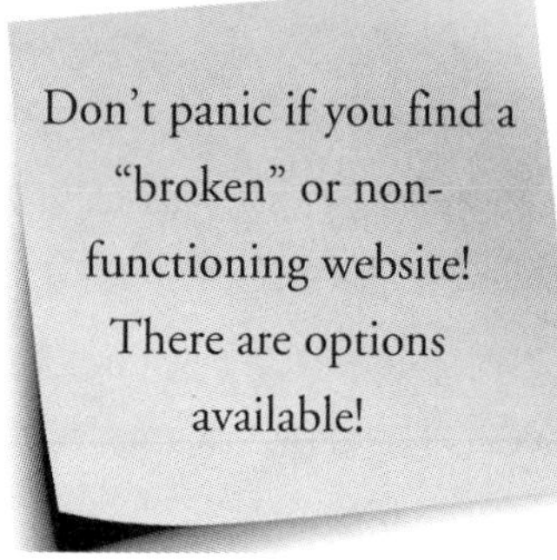

Don't panic if you find a
"broken" or non-
functioning website!
There are options
available!

If the error message you receive from Google is the 404 message (as shown above), you might also try checking *Google Cache*. You get that by clicking on your back button, until you reach the Google page where you launched your request. Once there, go to the same hit. At the end of the hit will be a link that says *Cached.* If you click on that, you'll be taken to the page as it was saved by Google. Google takes a snapshot of every page it locates, and stores (caches) that snapshot. Often, this will provide you with the information you are looking for.

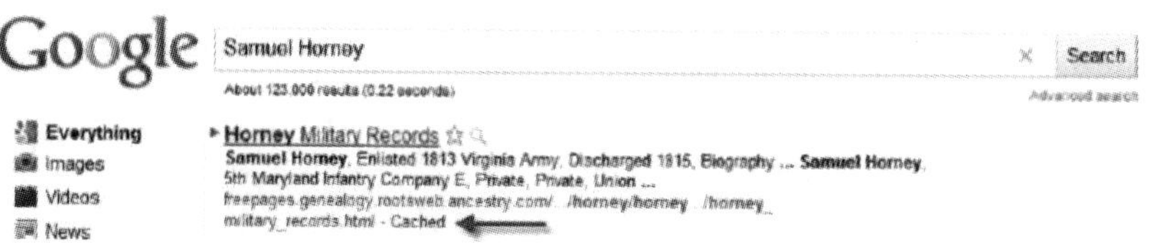

If that doesn't do the trick for you – I have another trick up my sleeve. As mentioned, snapshots are regularly taken of websites. Even when they have been taken down, you can often find them. Using the example from above, I tried a link that was a dead end: *http://iltrails.org/schuyler/oldsettlersbio1.html#47.* I trimmed it back slowly, trying it several times, with no luck. So I tried another tack. I went to *www.archive.org.* Once there, I pasted the URL into the *Wayback Machine* search engine and clicked on *Search.* I was provided with a chart of dates when the website had been up and working. All I needed to do was click the latest date available, and I was rewarded with a copy of the website from that earlier date – almost magic!

I clicked on the latest date available, and found the website that contained the information I was looking for – information I once thought was lost, but was now found. (**Note** – it was this newly discovered biography, that I found from February 21, 2005, from which I was able to share the biography of Samuel Horney earlier in this chapter in the *Local Histories* section.)

Had I entered the information in the *Wayback Machine* and gotten an error message (it happens sometimes!), I could have tried trimming back the URL. It may have brought me to a main page for the website, and I'd have been able to then find the working link to the website.

5. FREE SERVICES

If you're like me, you always gravitate to free things first. I like to go grocery shopping on Saturdays so I can enjoy the free samples in the supermarket, I love those "buy-one-get-one-free" sales, etc. If you don't already know, there are a number of subscription services out there that cost from a few pennies to a few quarters a day. We'll talk about those later, but this chapter will cover some of the free sites I like best in doing my genealogy.

Cemetery Websites

There are a number of cemetery websites that are free. Some are better than others, but they are certainly a lot easier – and cheaper — to peruse than hopping in your car for a cross-country trip.

Some cemetery websites feature photographs of tombstones. Many – most – offer abstracts – transcriptions – of the information on websites. New cemetery websites are coming online daily, so it is good to check frequently, especially if you have been unsuccessful in finding information online in the past for a particular cemetery or town. While writing this book, I typed *cemeteries online* into Google. I was rewarded with 1.3 million hits! So, you may want to narrow your search a bit by typing the name of a town, county or state.

Several lines of my family go back to Schuyler County, Illinois. I know from several things I have read online that members of my family were buried in the Thompson Cemetery that is found in Littleton Township, Schuyler

County, Illinois. So I went to my trusty search engine and typed *Schuyler County Cemeteries, Littleton, Illinois.* I was greeted by a number of links, one of which was a listing of all cemeteries in Schuyler County, Illinois, one of which was the Thompson Cemetery. As I clicked on that link, I was delighted to find that someone had visited the cemetery, transcribed all the headstones in the small family cemetery, and posted them on the Internet. In addition, this genealogy friend had posted additional genealogical information about many of the individuals buried there. There were many tombstones included in the table, with death dates ranging between 1838 and 1913. Since this was a family cemetery, I was related to all of these individuals, and numerous were direct-line ancestors! What a find.

Some of the more popular cemetery websites are:

http://www.ancestorsatrest.com/cemetery_records/ — *Ancestors at Rest* has a large database containing many free death records: coffin plates, funeral cards, death cards, wills, memorial cards, cemeteries, vital stats, obituaries, church records, family Bibles, cenotaphs and tombstone inscriptions. **Note**: this is a subscription service.

www.usgennet.org/usa/topic/cemetery/ — This site, sponsored by the American History and Genealogy Project (AHGP), provides transcriptions and photos for cemeteries throughout the United States.

www.findagrave.com – This website grew out of the passion of one individual (Jim Tipton) who was fascinated by graves, and began collecting and posting information about the graves of famous people. His work is now aided and abetted by over 500,000 volunteer contributors. Several of the links lead you to sites that are subscription-based, but many others do not. They boast 34 million graves listed.

www.interment.net – This is a free online library of burial records from thousands of cemeteries across the world, for historical and genealogy research.

www3.sympatico.ca/bkinnon/cemeteries.htm –This search engine serves as a gateway to a number of free cemetery transcription websites.

www.usgennet.org/usa/topic/cemetery/ — US Gen Net is a non-profit historical-genealogical web hosting service on the Internet.

www.usgwtombstones.org — The purpose of this project is to organize volunteers who will work together to create a lasting tribute to ancestors. Volunteers will transcribe tombstone inscriptions and have that work archived for the future and made easily accessible to all.

Don't forget –
cemeteries are a great
place to find your
ancestors!

These are just a few of the many – hundreds / thousands – of cemetery websites. As mentioned earlier, many of them have photos of tombstones, but many more merely have transcriptions of the tombstones. Regardless, they are great sites to visit to glean genealogical information.

Ellis Island

If you have ancestors that immigrated to America, and if they came by boat between 1892 and 1954, then the Ellis Island website (*www.ellisisland.org* – note the .org and not .com!) will be of interest to you. In fact, if you are living in America, there's a pretty good chance that at least one of your ancestors arrived on the shores of America from Europe. Many of those ships arrived in American cities that required immigration screening and clearance. Ellis Island is probably the most famous, owing, perhaps, to an over-active public relations agent. Or, it could be because approximately 12,500,000 immigrants went through the gates of Ellis Island as their first step and experience with America. But – and this is important – over three times that number entered the United States through other, lesser-known ports. So, if you are looking for an ancestor who immigrated to America between 1820 and 1920 and they are not found on the Ellis Island website, don't be discouraged – they can still be found, as records were kept at each of the other ports. Most records from other ports aren't yet online, and while that's a shame, I believe that over time most will make their appearance online. In addition to Ellis Island, the following ports were used by immigrants entering the US between 1820 and 1920:

Baltimore, MD – 1,460,000
Boston, MA — 2,050,000
Charleston, SC – 20,000
Galveston, TX – 110,000
Key West, FL – 130,000
New Bedford, MA – 40,000
New York City, NY – 23,960,000
New Orleans, LA – 710,000
Passamaquoddy, Maine – 80,000
Philadelphia, PA – 1,240,000
Portland / Falmouth, ME – 120,000
Providence, RI – 40,000
San Francisco, CA – 500,000

As you can see, the top ports in order of arrival in the United States were:

New York
Boston
Baltimore

Remember – not all immigrants came though Ellis Island!

Philadelphia
New Orleans
San Francisco

And, we can't forget Castle Garden, the predecessor to Ellis Island. It was the first point of arrival for 11,000,000 immigrants between 1830 and 1892, the year that Ellis Island opened.

Ellis Island (known by Italian immigrants as *Isola della Lacrime* – The Island of Tears) is without question one of my favorite websites to play around with. As you search for your ancestors, you'll be amazed at the user friendliness of the website, the information contained there, and the ease with which you can move around.

As mentioned, Ellis Island opened for business in 1892. It served the immigrating folks well until it closed down in 1954.

So let's take a quick tour of the Ellis Island website. The first thing you'll see on the welcome page is a search engine where you'll want to put the name of an ancestor. If you're not certain of the first name, or perhaps uncertain about the spelling of the first name, then simply enter the surname of the individual(s) you are looking for, along with an approximate year of birth. You can leave that blank, if you wish.

Many of my ancestors came to America prior to Ellis Island's operation. But for grins, let's see if we can find some of them. I know my Quillen ancestor – Teague McQuillan – originated in County Antrim, Ireland (now part of Northern Ireland). Teague came to America in the 1630s, so of course he won't be found on the Ellis Island website. But let's see if there are any

McQuillans that hailed from County Antrim who followed their ancestor to America. (It's a pretty sure deal they are related. The McQuillans had a knack of lining up on the wrong sides of battles, and the McQuillan Clan is quite small compared to other Irish clans. If the name's McQuillan, we're related!)

So we'll enter *McQuillan* into the website, leaving the first name blank. You'll immediately be greeted by a request to either sign in or register. Don't worry – there's no charge. They just like to keep track of who is perusing their website. I registered years ago, and I don't recall ever getting any spam e-mails from them. So go ahead – register.

After I register, the website comes back and gives me a list of nearly 300 McQuillans who entered the US through Ellis Island. I scan the list, noting those who came from County Antrim. For fun, I selected Philip McQuillan, who came to America from Belfast, Ireland (Northern Ireland did not exist as an entity until 1922) in 1915. Clicking on his name (which is linked to his passenger record), the following information appears:

Name: Philip McQuillan
Ethnicity: Britain
Place of Residence: Belfast, Ireland
Date of Arrival: October 31, 1915
Age on Arrival: 33 years
Gender: Male
Marital Status: Single
Ship of Travel: New York
Port of Departure: Liverpool, England

This summary for Philip provides me with some basic information about him. I learn that his residence is Belfast, that he was 33 years old in 1915 (which makes his birth date 1881 or 1882), and that he is single.

On the same page where this information is displayed, there are several nice options, especially if you know or believe this passenger is an ancestor. If you click on the button that says *View Original Ship Manifest,* you will be taken to a page with a digital image of the actual passenger list where your ancestor's name is written. As I view that page, I can almost envision this person, waiting his turn in a very long line, as he approaches a small table with an overworked shipping company employee. The employee scarcely looks up at my relative, and just rattles off the questions he has for him. Sometimes he has to ask my ancestor to repeat his answer, because his Irish brogue is so thick.

Okay – back to the ship's manifest. The picture of the page can be enlarged (look for the small icon of a magnifying glass just to the right of the image), and a veritable genealogical treasure awaits you.

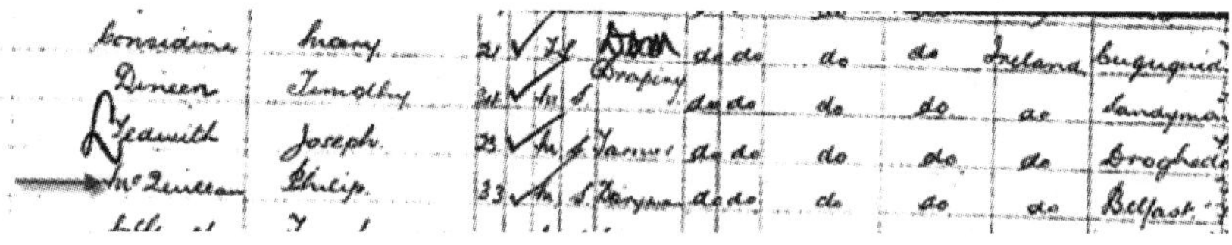

Note: Sometimes it seems like you have entered in the middle of a page. Well, you have. Depending on the year of immigration, the ship's manifest was either on one very large page, or two facing pages. If the latter, then a digital image was taken and posted of each page separately. If you can't find your ancestor's name (it should be on one of the first columns on the left), go back a page on the Internet, then request *Previous Page*. Then you'll be able to find your ancestor. But be sure to note the line # he or she is on, as you'll want to go to the second page to see the remaining questions and answers.

The ship's manifest collected an amazing (and sometimes startling!) set of facts about the individual, including some wonderful genealogical clues. Many of the questions are similar to those found on the US Census. The ship manifest questions changed somewhat from year to year, but regardless of the year, they provide interesting information on each passenger. In 1915, the questions asked (and answered) were:

- Were they a citizen, diplomat, tourist, or a citizen of Canada, China or Mexico?
- What was their age in years and months?
- What was their sex and marital status?
- What was their occupation, and could they read and write?
- What was their nationality and race?
- What was their last permanent address?
- What was the name and complete residence address of a relative or friend in the country from whence they came?
- What was the passenger's final destination (state and town)?
- Did they have a ticket to their final destination?
- Who paid the passage for this individual?
- Did they have at least $50? If not, how much did they have?
- Had they been to the United States before, and if so, where and for how long?
- Were they coming to visit a relative or friend? And if so, who was it and what was their full address?
- Were they a polygamist?

•Were they an Anarchist?
•What was their mental and physical health condition?
•Were they deformed or crippled, and if so, the nature, length of time and cause?
•Did they have any identifying marks?
•What was their height, complexion and color of hair and eyes?
•Where was their place of birth?

You can see why some of this information would make a genealogist's heart flutter! In the case of Philip McQuillan, in addition to what we learned on the summary page (his age, marital status, residence, and place of departure), we learn that he was:

•a dairyman;
•from Belfast;
•the son of William McQuillan of Fairview Glen Road in Belfast;
•going to see his brother, James McQuillan, who lived on Liberty Avenue in Pittsburgh, Pennsylvania;
•not a polygamist or anarchist (thank goodness!);
•had no "deformities" or identifying marks;
•5'-3" with a light complexion, brown hair and blue eyes;
•born in Belfast.

A treasure load of genealogical information indeed! Not only do I know more about Philip, but I know his father's name, his brother's name and the city where he lives in America.

If you're interested, for a few shekels you can order a copy of the ship's manifest.

Also available to view and/or purchase is a photograph of the ship in which your ancestor crossed the Atlantic, coming to his or her new life. Back on the web page that listed the summary of the passenger's information is a label entitled *View Ship*. Just click on that label and *voila* – there is the picture of the ship. For example, here's the ship in which Philip travelled, named the *City of New York*:

As you learn about the Ellis Island website, you'll find for yourself how easy it is to navigate and to find individuals. Like using other search engines, be sure not to get focused on one spelling or your ancestor's name. Be open to other options. McQuillan could be McQuillan, McQuillin, McQuillon, McQuillian, etc.

FamilySearch.org

If you do much genealogy online, sooner than later – and probably sooner than later — you will run into the genealogy website hosted by the Church of Jesus Christ of Latter-day Saints (the LDS Church / Mormons) called

FamilySearch™. This website has incredibly deep genealogical pockets, and boasts the genealogy records of millions – nearly a billion! — of people from all over the world. The site is free, open to individuals of all faiths (or no faith, for that matter!) as a public service to the world's population.

If you have never used FamilySearch before, I would invite you to go to it and just play around, familiarizing yourself with its operations, the various collections they have, etc. There are so many aspects of the website, and the simplicity of the home page belies the incredible volume of information that awaits you. Beyond more than the millions of genealogical records available, the website also offers online classes in genealogy, a research wiki, tutorials on how to get started, how to overcome roadblocks, etc. In early 2011, the LDS Church announced that they had just *added* 72,000,000 (yes – that's 72 *million*) genealogy records to their online collection!

Let's do a quick search for one of my relatives. You have met him before – Jonathan Baldwin Quillen, my second-great grandfather. Go to FamilySearch.org. From there, I enter Jonathan's name in the boxes at the top of the page.

Discover Your Family History

Historical Records Family Trees Library Catalog

First Names: Jonathan
Last Name: Quillen

Place:
From Year: 1845
To Year: 1920

Search Advanced search

When I hit *Search*, I get the following results:

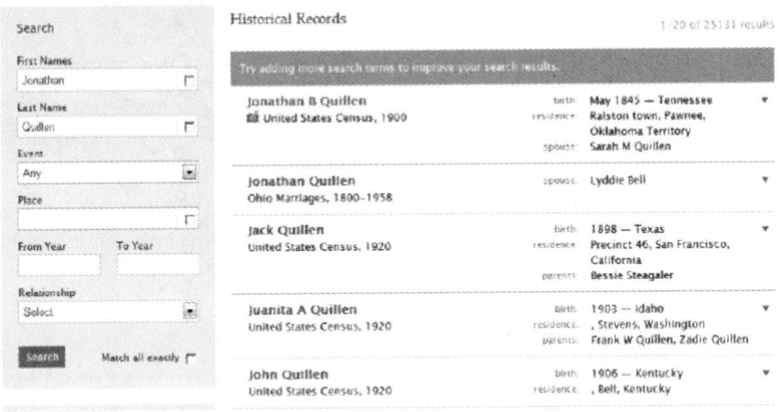

You may note that we received over 25,000 hits on my request! That's a few to have to pour through, even for avid and driven genealogists!

Back on the first page, you'll note the link called *Advanced Search*. If I know a little more about this person (which I happen to!), I can improve my chances of finding records more specific for my ancestor:

Historical Records Family Trees Library Catalog

First Names: Jonathan — Last Name: Quillen

Event: Birth — Place: Tennessee — Year: 1845 — +/-: 5

Relationship: Spouse — First Names: Sarah — Last Name:

Search — Basic search — Match all terms exactly

If I add the additional information I have for Jonathan, the search will be narrowed to (hopefully) a more manageable number of hits. The Event box allows me to enter *Birth, Residence, Marriage* or *Death*, and then provides additional boxes for that information. The *Relationship* box allows me to enter *Spouse* or *Parents*, and provides boxes for their names. Also, in the box marked +/-, you have the opportunity to look for dates within 1, 2, 5, 10 or 20 years from the date you entered. With this information loaded in, the search narrowed potential records to about 4,500 records – much more manageable (but still a lot of records).

However, it singled out those that FamilySearch thought were the closest and most likely hits. As it turns out, each of the hits above the box that says "*The following results…*" is a record about this second-great grandfather of mine. (Note that all the records are from the US Census from three different decades. Note also that his birth date is listed as 1845, 1846 and 1849. More on that later!)

Once I have hits that I think belong to this ancestor of mine, I can click on the individual's name, and I will be taken to the record that shows more

about him or her. You'll note that some of the records have the icon of a camera next to them. This indicates that they have images available of that particular record. For those records that don't have that icon, there is a transcription of the information.

As mentioned earlier, beyond being able to search for your ancestors, FamilySearch.org provides a wide variety of tutorials and tools for genealogists: free online classes in genealogy, a research wiki, tutorials on how to get started, how to overcome roadblocks, etc.

FamilySearch.org is a powerful website and you must spend time on it.

FAMILYSEARCH VOLUNTEER OPPORTUNITIES!

FamilySearch has an army of volunteers continually working on expanding their collections and getting those collections online so the general public can benefit from them. Their projects are almost always in need of volunteers. On the FamilySearch.org home page, look for the *Give Back* tab at the top of the page. Clicking that takes you to a page that describes opportunities available for volunteers. The *Indexing* tab at the top of the page also provides you with information on how you can go about volunteering.

Because of the work of hordes of volunteers, many records are able to be added to FamilySearch's collection for everyone to benefit from. Most recently they have added new searchable image collections to the site, including the first Chinese collection, which consists of nearly 18.5 million records – birth, death, marriage, pedigrees, etc. Collections have also been added for Belgium, Germany, Guatemala, Mexico, Netherlands, Philippines and Puerto Rico.

Ancestry.com Message Boards

You may be wondering why I have Ancestry.com Message Boards as part of the free section of genealogy resources. Ancestry costs money, right? Well, yes it does, but as a service to its followers (1.7 *million* subscribers at last count!), Ancestry provides their message boards free of charge, as do other genealogy websites. From what I can tell, Ancestry's is the biggest. It can serve as a great teaser for you to subscribe to Ancestry.com.

I have used many message boards, and Ancestry's are the ones I find the most traffic on. Other free message boards can be found on *Cyndislist.com, Rootsweb.com, GenForum.com, Genealogy.com, MyHeritage.com*, etc. Just Google genealogy *message boards*, and you'll find many that are out there, including some that are surname-specific. To find message boards specific to the surname you are searching, just add the surname at the beginning of the search string: *Quillen genealogy message boards.*

Libraries

I have listed libraries in the free section, because many (most) public libraries have subscribed to a number of genealogy services, typically *Ancestry.com* and *HeritageQuest.com.* A visit to their genealogy section will generally allow you to find computers that can be used for accessing the library's subscription services. Some services – particularly HeritageQuest.com – allow their services to be accessed via the Internet, through the library's website. Such a deal! It generally takes a library card for that library, and you are set to go. Some library websites list their genealogy tools – such as HeritageQuest – on their home page, and other times they are several layers below the home page. The Denver Public Library, for example, lists *Western History and Genealogy* on their home page. Clicking that link brings you to the online

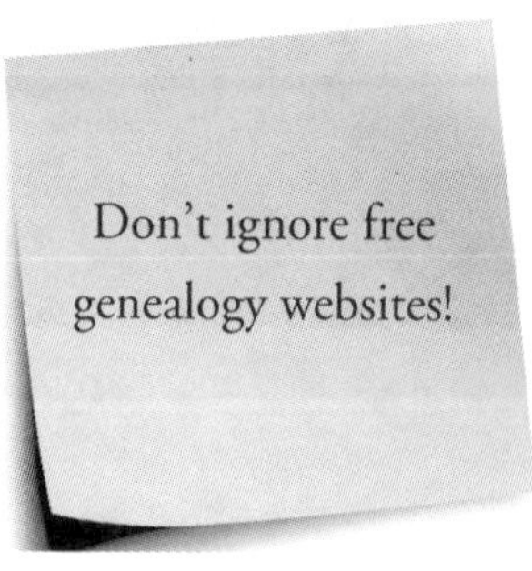
Don't ignore free genealogy websites!

genealogy tools they have, including HeritageQuest. Just a few clicks and I was able to view the 1900 census page for Jonathan and his family. Isn't technology great!?

Even smaller libraries often offer these services. For fun and out of curiosity (and for this book), I went to the website for the library in the small berg of Rushville, Illinois (population 3,212) where one line of my family hails from. On the front page was the following pronouncement:

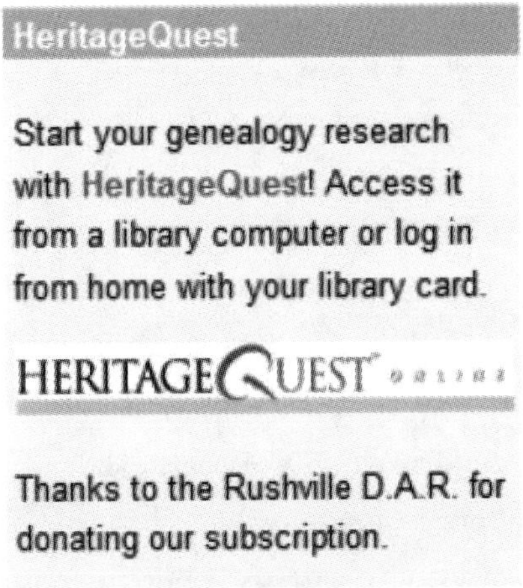

HeritageQuest

Start your genealogy research with HeritageQuest! Access it from a library computer or log in from home with your library card.

HERITAGEQUEST

Thanks to the Rushville D.A.R. for donating our subscription.

So don't overlook libraries as a point of access to online genealogy tools.

USGenWeb

USGenWeb is a marvelous free online tool. I like it because it embodies one of the key characteristics of genealogists – the spirit of volunteerism. It is a massive, nationwide undertaking, and relies on thousands of volunteers for the information on their websites. The opening paragraph on their home page says:

> Welcome to The USGenWeb Project! We are a group of volunteers working together to provide free genealogy websites for genealogical research in every county and every state of the United States. This project is non-commercial and fully committed to free genealogy access for everyone.

The projects are at state and county level. I have yet to run across a county that hasn't had at least one volunteer (normally there are many) working on it. I suppose it is conceivable that with so many counties nationwide, there may be a few that do not (yet) have volunteers, but I haven't run across one yet. Because it is all volunteer, the quality and quantity of information varies widely. Some counties have volumes and volumes of information, while others have much more scanty information provided.

And what kinds of information are provided? There appears to be no standard format or requirement, but you may find online information for marriages, births, deaths, land records, tombstone transcriptions, journal entries, etc., etc. Some records are transcribed, others provide the digital images.

UsGenWeb is a tremendous site that may be a valuable tool for you in your research. So don't overlook www.usgenweb.com.

RootsWeb.com

Another favorite free website I have used and enjoy is RootsWeb.ancestry.com (*www.rootsweb.com*). As happens often, it has been subsumed into the Ancestry.com dynasty. But, this portion is still free, and provides genealogy tutorials, access to various search engines and databases (such as the Social Security Death Index), family trees, message boards and a plethora of other cool sites to visit. There is also an area where you can get copies of various downloadable forms and charts (pedigree charts, family group sheets, census templates, etc). It's a very helpful site to visit and poke around on.

Cyndi's List

No genealogy book would be complete without a reference to the mega-genealogy site Cyndi's List (*www.cyndislist.com*). Oh my goodness. This site is huge, with links that run every which way. It is so large that I sometimes get overwhelmed with the amount of information available and options that confront me. Their latest home page boasts they have over 291,000 genealogy links! That's a lot of ancestors. I will tell you straight up that you have to work a lot with Cyndi's List to become familiar with its navigation, organization and how best to get the most out of the website.

I am not sure how long Cyndi's List has been available, but I first became aware of this site over a decade ago, and I have used it frequently in the intervening years.

6. SUBSCRIPTION SERVICES

Unlike the services featured in the previous chapter, the services shared in this chapter are subscription services, requiring monthly, quarterly or annual subscriptions.

Ancestry.com

Okay, I have a confession to make. I am not a swearing man (I suppose that's not a *confession*, but more of an *admission*), but for several years every time I came upon a website emblazoned with Ancestry.com's leaf-design logo,

I wanted to find someone who could teach me to swear.

In the previous chapter I admitted I really like free services, and for years I did my genealogy by using many of the free websites that are listed in that chapter, scrupulously avoiding – even shunning — those that cost money. But often, even the free websites I used seemed to have been co-opted – as I followed a thread through various internet sites, I would eventually get to that blasted Ancestry logo – and could go no further without a subscription.

I am over that now. I have realized that the information provided by Ancestry is incredibly voluminous and is not too difficult to find. Who am I to begrudge someone from making a buck or two for working really hard to make my life easier? So a few years ago I went over to the dark side, and have actually begun using numerous of these subscription services on a regular basis. While Ancestry.com is the 800-pound gorilla in the genealogy rain forest, there are a number of other worthwhile subscription services that you might consider. (By the way, did you know that the largest Mountain Gorilla on record was 590 pounds?)

Ancestry.com is reputed to have approximately five billion records in their vast collection. 5,000,000,000. That's a lot of names, if you ask me. And a lot of places that you may be able to find those ancestors of yours, even the most frustratingly elusive ones.

The only complaint I have is that, for whatever reason, Ancestry seems compelled to provide me with about any hit that is even remotely similar to the information for which I am seeking. Even when I use their *Advance Search* capabilities, similar-but-clearly-different information is provided. For example, if I search for records that might confirm that my second-great grandfather, Jonathan Baldwin Quillen, was born in 1845 in Tennessee, I get 38,226 hits. Really? Uh, no. Of those, 3,347 are to be found in censuses. So I check the census, and I am given hits for Nancy J. Quillen, born in Alabama, Eliza Quillen born in Virginia, and so on. They do set apart those that are a closer match, and that is nice, but the extra 38,220 hits are a little annoying! I will admit that sometimes I'll find him mixed into that 38,226 hits under a slightly different misspelling; but you'd really have to misspell pretty badly to mistake Nancy J. Quillen for Jonathan Baldwin Quillen!

Okay – thank you. It was good to get that off my chest.

Ancestry.com has massive collections of information and is an incredibly valuable tool for searching out your ancestors. There are also nice additions like tutorials, how to get started, getting the most out of XYZ types of records, DNA research, collaboration (sharing your genealogy), message boards, etc. They were among the first to put censuses online so that you could view the actual images.

The free market has helped grow Ancestry's offerings. As free websites continue to put more and more records online, Ancestry must keep a few steps ahead of them and other subscription sites, so they are very active in adding to their collections. On their home page, they have a section called *What's Happening at Ancestry.com*, where they list new records and collections that have recently come on line. They always have eight to a dozen on the home page, and then another page that lists all their new additions – very impressive.

Ancestry.com's rates for US research are $12.95/month for an annual subscription ($155.40 annually), $16.95 per month for a three-month subscription, and $19.95 per month for a monthly subscription. The three- and 12-month subscriptions are billed all at one time. Ancestry.com offers a 14-day free trial if you want a test drive first. Subscriptions that allow access to non-US records (like Canadian and British censuses, for example) are more expensive.

If you cannot afford to pay these subscription fees, don't lose heart! As mentioned earlier in the *Free Services* section, many public libraries subscribe to one or both of these services, so you may be able to access them as close as your local library.

Notwithstanding my resistance in the early years, and a few concerns I mentioned above, Ancestry.com is one of my favorite genealogy services. In fact, if I could afford to subscribe to only one service, Ancestry.com would be that service.

Fold3.com

If Ancestry.com is my favorite subscription service, Fold3.com (*www.fold3.com*) is a close second. (Note: Fold3.com was formerly known as Footnote.com before it joined the Ancestry.com covey of companies in 2010.) It is a tremendous service, with large collections. Like Ancestry, it suffers a bit from trying to provide too many hits for any given search, and sometimes navigation is a bit of a challenge, but I have been mostly very impressed with their offering.

Free is good. Subscriptions are good too; they just cost more.

In the research I have been doing in recent years, I have come to appreciate Fold3's immigration and naturalization collection, which is far superior to any of their competition – whether free or fee.

Through years of using both Fold3 and Ancestry, I have determined that each has strengths in their collections, as well as weaknesses. For example, while Fold3 has the most extensive collection of immigration and naturalization records, Ancestry.com's military records collection far surpasses Fold3's military collection. At any rate – that was the case when Ancestry purchased Footnote. With Fold3's expressed desire to focus in military records, its military holdings may soon overtake Ancestry's lead in that area of records. Trial and error, and familiarization with each service will help you determine which you should use when searching for your ancestors. At the time of this writing, there are two levels of service: the first is free, and it provides access to many records. However for full access to their online records, a subscription to Fold3 will run you $11.95 a month, or $79.95 for an annual subscription.

Together, Ancestry.com and Fold3.com form an awesome one-two punch when it comes to searching for your ancestors. Add to them FamilySearch.com and you've got a preponderance of genealogical records at your fingertips.

Decide which combination of services works best for the information I need.

Genealogy.com

Like Fold3.com, Genealogy.com (*www.genealogy.com*) has become part

of the Ancestry.com family. They have been around for years, and like other subscription services, provide a wide range of genealogy collections and services. message boards, tutorials (I love these!), forums, and various and sundry genealogy collections are available through their service.

There are three levels of annual subscriptions to Genealogy.com. They are the Gold membership ($199.99), Deluxe Membership ($99.99) and Basic Membership ($69.99). All of the subscriptions include *Family Tree Maker* genealogy software, a nice perq that comes with the subscription. Each level of membership comes with a 14-day free trial, but you have to provide your credit card information to get even the free trial. While you can cancel with no cost (prior to the subscription starting), it's a hassle that kind of miffs me.

As their names indicate, each level of membership provides greater access to their collections. The Basic and Deluxe memberships are so close in price that I would opt for the Deluxe. It provides access to their World Family Tree while the Basic membership does not. Neither of the lower two subscriptions allow access to censuses, which seems odd to me. To get access to censuses, you need the Gold membership.

Newspaper Archives

I covered this website (*www.newspaperarchive.com*) in the *Searching* chapter. Newspapers are a wonderful source for use when you need to go beyond the main records where many ancestors are often found – censuses, military records, immigration and naturalization records, etc. Besides, it's fun to read print from by-gone eras. The subscription rates are much less ($6.00 to $10.00 a month, depending on whether you want a monthly or annual subscription) than other general subscription services.

One Great Family

One Great Family (*www.onegreatfamily.com*) is a massive site that features one of the greatest on-going collaboration projects in the genealogy world. Their website says that they are: "…a cooperative effort between you and the rest of the world." They work to store and link overlapping family trees, world-wide. As their website adds, it allows you to leverage your work with the work many others are doing on your ancestral lines. They even suggest that you need no other genealogy software – they provide all the services you need on their Internet-based application. While that may be true, I think I will keep my own software on my own PC, thank you! But – it is an intriguing thought.

One Great Family's press kit indicates that approximately 400,000 new names are added *weekly* to their database – that's a lot of potential ancestors!

Subscription fees are pretty reasonable – approximately $10 for a month, $20 to $30 for a quarterly subscription or $60 to $80 for an annual subscription. (Note – the ranges depend on whether you catch them when they are having a sale, or if you pay full price.) Quarterly and annual subscriptions are paid in one lump sum. A seven-day free trial is available, although, like several other subscription services, you must provide your credit card number, then remember to unsubscribe before the trial period ends.

World Vital Records

World Vital Records (*www.worldvitalrecords.com)* has been around for a number of years. They have existed primarily in the shadow of Ancestry.com (most have), but are still a viable option for doing genealogy research. World Vital Records offers US and international databases for researchers to peruse.

World Vital Records has two basic levels of subscription – one for US databases and one for international databases. Both offer a seven-day free trial, but you have to provide your credit card to get the trial, then remember to cancel is prior to the end of the trial. US access is available for $40 annually, and international access is available for $99 per year. The international subscription includes US records.

HeritageQuest

If you have done genealogy at your local library, you may be familiar with HeritageQuest (*www.heritagequest.com*), since many libraries (over 2,600 at last count) have subscriptions for their patrons to use. Their collection isn't as extensive as some others that are mentioned here, but they include censuses, over 26,000 family and local histories, periodicals (over 2.1 million articles), Revolutionary War records, and the Freedman's Bank for African-Americans.

With a few clicks of my mouse, I was able to access HeritageQuest from home, and, searching their *Revolutionary War* section, find the digital images of a number of records about my fifth-great grandfather, John Quillin, of Cumberland County, North Carolina. One of those records was his sworn testimony about his service during the Revolutionary War, given in his 76th year of age, so that he might obtain a pension for his service. It was rich in genealogical information, some of it – like his birth date and place of birth – was over 250 years old. You gotta love genealogy! The document included "his mark" – instead of his signature:

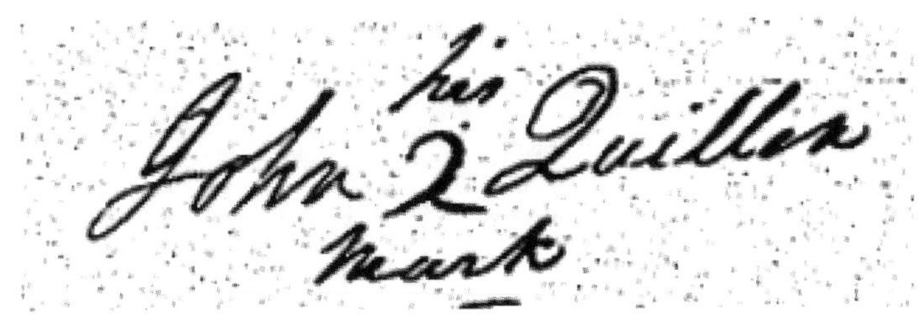

Based on other "marks" I have seen, I believe his mark, unlike the X of legend, was a cursive Q – which looks a bit like the number 2. Based on a handwriting comparison with the rest of the document, I believe the clerk then wrote my ancestor's name – given name before and surname after his mark – and included the words *his* and *mark* above and below the mark. And best of all – I discovered all this while sitting at my desk at home.

I was a little unsure where to list HeritageQuest – whether in the *Free Services* or *Subscription Services* chapters. It is a subscription service for libraries, but HeritageQuest doesn't provide subscriptions to individuals. As you can see, I decided to include it in the *Subscription Services* chapter, although I did give it a nod in the *Libraries* section of the *Free Services* chapter.

Even though you are excited about genealogy now, be careful how many subscription services you sign up for, and for how long!

As noted, most of these subscription services offer free trials, typically for either seven or fourteen days. If you are venturing into subscription services for the first time, I would suggest taking full advantage of these trial offers, even though you have to provide your credit card number and remember to cancel before the trial is over. Also, even though you are really excited about doing genealogy (I believe and understand that!), be careful about the length of subscription for which you sign up. I have been doing genealogy for years, and as passionate as I am about it, sometimes months will go by and I haven't touched it. That's okay – that's one of the cool things about doing genealogy – but it's unfortunate if you have one or more subscription services sitting out there going unused, although you are paying for them. Be cautious, don't over buy. Or – don't be like me and my fated exercise programs. I get into an exercise pattern and get all excited. I decide to buy a year's membership, because maybe the cost of the membership will help me stay motivated. If you are like me…Bad Plan. Very Bad Plan. Once that check is written, within a week or two the motivation that the purchase provided is gone. The motivation has to come from elsewhere, at least for me!

There are of course many other fee-based genealogy services, but based on my research experience, those listed here are the most common you will run into.

7. GOVERNMENT RECORDS

Okay – like most Americans, when it comes down to it, I don't mind paying taxes. Yes, I think I am taxed too much, but fundamentally I agree with the concept. I like the national interstate system. I like having a standing military to defend me and my family. I like a lot of those things. I also love many of the records the federal and state governments have commissioned and kept from the earliest beginnings of our country. Censuses, military service records, immigration and naturalization records, land records, marriage, birth and death records, and so on and so forth. Because the government has kept and preserved these records through the generations, the efforts of genealogists are often rewarded with success. In this chapter, we'll spend a little time with each of the records mentioned above.

Censuses

Within a dozen years of the establishment of the United States, Congress commissioned the first census of its citizens. And they set the requirement that on the first year of each decade, another census would be taken of each state. The earliest censuses listed only the names of the heads of household, along with the age ranges and sex of the members of each family. For example, here is the census for my third-great grandfather from the 1830 US Census for Tuscarora Township, Mifflin County, Pennsylvania:

Head of Family: Joseph Cunningham
2 males under 5 years, 0 females under five years
2 males 5 to 10 years, 1 female 5 to 10 years

2 males 10 to 15 years, 0 females 10 to 15 years
0 males 15 to 20 years, 1 female 15 to 20 years
1 male 30 to 40 years, 1 female 30 to 40 years

So for this family of ten, we learn that:
— Joseph, the head of the household, was 30 to 40 years of age;
— his wife was also 30 to 40 years of age;
— they had six sons and two daughters in the age ranges provided.

As I work on genealogical research, it is interesting, intriguing and sometimes not a little frustrating following these families back through the years from census to census.

Since (and including) the 1850 census, every census has included the names and ages of each and every person living at that location at that time. As the years progressed, the government added questions to the list of data that was being requested. Much of that information is a boon to genealogists. Consider some of the questions that were added through the years (the year in parenthesis is the census year the question first appeared):

— Age (1850)
— # of slaves (1800)
— Foreigners not naturalized (1820)
— Birth place (1850)
— Married within the year (1850)
— Cannot read or write (1850)
— Father foreign born (1870)
— Mother foreign born (1870)
— Month born in census year (1870)
— Age June 1 in census year (1880)
— Relationship to head of house (1880)

— Single, married, widowed, divorced (1880)
— Place of birth of father (1880)
— Place of birth of mother (1880)
— Month of birth (1900)
— Year of birth (1900)
— Number of years married (1900)
— Number of children (1900)
— How many of these children living (1900)
— Years of immigration to US (1900)
— Number of years in US (1900)
— Naturalization (1900)
— Naturalized or alien (1910)
— Language spoken (1910)
— Civil War Veteran (1910)
— Mother tongue of father (1920)
— Mother tongue of mother (1920)
— Age at first marriage (1930)
— Were a veteran of US military or Naval forces (1930)
— What war or expedition (1930)

Other questions came and went, like whether individuals could read or write, did they attend school in the last year, occupation, did they own a radio, did they rent or own, value of real estate, etc. But these listed above provide assistance to genealogists as they search for their ancestors. The other questions add color and are interesting, but don't generally have genealogical value.

Owing to national privacy protection laws, the latest census available is the 1940 census. The 1950 census will be available in 2022 – so genealogists have will have to wait awhile for that!

Censuses can be a tremendous asset and resource for genealogists. They are readily accessible – both through free and subscription services – and contain a massive amount of data. Most are indexed, so gone are the days of slowly and carefully reading pages upon pages of census sheets. But the accessibility and volume of the data are two of the things that can make them a real pain in the proverbial side of genealogists. The reason? The vast majority of the information provided is considered a secondary source of information. It is information provided after the fact. Even the age of one of the residents of a home is subject to question. Did the person fib about their age, either during the visit with the census enumerator, or years before, and the fib continued to be perpetuated to the enumerator? Places of birth can't be counted on, because the person probably doesn't know for certain. Memories fade. Was it Jenny that was born in Mifflin County, or was it Sarah? Did we move the year before she was born or after? And so forth and so on.

Perhaps a short tutorial on how censuses were enumerated is helpful. The earliest census enumerators were often the same fellow who was asked to gather information for tax purposes. As the population grew and more questions were asked, separate census enumerators were employed. Enumerators were expected to go to each dwelling and ask questions of the residents of the household. They were typically paid *per capita* – so much per person, family and dwelling. For the 1900 census, enumerators were paid two cents per person, fifteen cents for each farm visited, with a supposed to speak with, in order of preference: the head of household, the spouse of the head of household, the eldest child, preferably one who was at least a teenager.

Learn the strengths *and* weaknesses of censuses!

minimum of $3.00 and a maximum of $6.00 per day. The enumerator was Enumerators then were as some people are now. Some may have cut corners, either of necessity of out of laziness, greed, a scary dog, or any of an infinite number of reasons. So a ten-year old may have provided information about her parents, their ages, birth places, etc. Or an adult neighbor might have been asked about the family that lived up the hollow – did they know them, their ages, places of birth, etc?

How else do you explain the discrepancies that appear when researching censuses. Let's use my second-great grandfather as an example. As I was writing this book, I jumped on several genealogy websites to get information on him. Here's what I found on Jonathan Baldwin Quillen on consecutive censuses:

Census	**Name**	**Age**	**Year of Birth**	**Place of Birth**
1860	Johnathan Qulline	12	1848	Sullivan County, Tennessee
1870	Jonathan Quillan	21	1849	Sullivan County, Tennessee
1880	J.B. Quillen	31	1849	Tennessee
1900	Jonathan B. Quillen	55	May 1845	Tennessee
1910	John B. Quillen	64	1846	Tennessee

Because of the other people in the various records – parents, siblings, wife, children, I know this is all the same man — Jonathan Baldwin Quillen. But note the variations in the spellings of his names, as well as the variation in his birth years – in five censuses, his birth years are identified as 1845, 1846,

1848 and 1849. Note that his age increases 9, 10, 14 and 9 years, year over year. Since censuses were enumerated at roughly the same time each year in the first year of each decade, you would think his age would increment ten years each census.

At least his birth place remained the same. In censuses, his son, my great grandfather, has his birth place listed as Virginia and Tennessee – alternating between those two states over the years.

So – you see some of the foibles of censuses. Don't get me wrong – I am a big fan of using censuses in genealogical research. Just don't take everything you read there as the gospel truth. Use it as a clue to help you find other supporting records – primary sources — that will nail down some of that information that is so important to you.

You may note that the 1890 census is missing from the table of census information for my second-great grandfather. Sadly, a fire destroyed the vast majority of the 1890 census…ah – the data that was lost in that blaze! But all is not totally lost. In a collaborative effort between the federal government, Ancestry.com and the Allen County Public Library, an 1890 substitute census was created representing approximately 20 million Americans – about 30% of the US population in 1890. They pulled together the surviving fragments of the 1890 census, along with veterans' schedules, Native American Censuses (which were housed separately from the US censuses), 1885 and 1895 state censuses, city and county directories, voter registration lists and other documents to at least provide some information. Add to that the 1890 Oklahoma Indian Territory Census, and all is not completely lost.

Follow these steps to access the substitute 1890 census on Ancestry.com:
— from the Ancestry.com home page, hover your cursor over the *Search* tab

in the top center of the page. Then:

— on the menu, select *Card Catalog*

— under *Filter by Collection*, click on Census & Voter Lists

— Click on *1890s*

— under *Filter by Location*, click on *USA*

— Select *State*, then click on your state as it appears in the box

— you'll be taken to a page that lists the databases available for the state you selected. From there, you can search each database for the information you are seeking.

Don't overlook the records that ARE available from 1890, even though the 1890 Census was burned!

One final thought on the US Census: Whenever I find a member of my family in the census, I have found it useful to check the families that live near my family member – families often settled close to one another. A father might subdivide his land so that his son or daughter and their family could have land and a place to live. Below is a census page for my second-great grandfather, Jeremiah Hudson and his family. Three houses away is his father, my third-great grandfather — Francis Marion Hudson. When I find a family member in the census, I routinely check the census pages before and after the page on

State Censuses

In addition to the federal censuses which occurred the first year of each decade, many states conducted a state census. Many territories also conducted their own census prior to statehood. These censuses were typically conducted later in the decade. Since they were conducted later in the decade, in addition to the information they provide, they help genealogists more closely chart the movement of these families in a shorter time interval than ten years. Children could have been born and died – a common thing – between the federal censuses, and without state censuses, you might never know of their existence.

Some states conducted censuses repeatedly and on a set schedule, as did the federal government, and some states did not. If your ancestors lived in New York, for example – you are lucky. New York conducted state censuses in 1825, 1835, 1845, 1855, 1865, 1875, 1892, 1905, 1915, and 1925. In my home state of Colorado, however, no state censuses were conducted. They did, however, conduct 1860 and 1870 territorial censuses. Connecticut also conducted only one state census – and that a military census – in 1917.

There are a number of places on the Internet where you can discover whether your state has conducted state and/or territorial censuses. One of the best I have found is *www.researchguides.net/census/state.htm.* Even though this is a book on doing online genealogy, I'll share a book I have found that is tremendously helpful in learning about what is and is not available relative to state and territorial censuses. It is the *Red Book: American State, County & Town Sources*, Alice Eichholz (editor), (Ancestry Publishing, June 1, 2004). The Red Book provides state-by-state information on where to go to find information on censuses, land records, cemetery records, court, tax and probate records, military records, newspapers and periodicals.

Mortality Schedules

Another important and often overlooked source of information associated with the federal censuses is *Mortality Schedules*. For the 1850 through 1880 censuses, in addition to asking questions about those living in a particular residence, the enumerator also asked for information about those who had died during the year prior to the enumeration date of the census. Information gleaned included the deceased's name, age, sex, marital status, race, occupation, birth place, cause of death, length of illness, etc.

While one year's worth of death data may not seem like much, it represents 10% of the deaths that occurred in the previous decade. It may be just enough to help you find someone who has been eluding you for years, or may even identify someone you knew nothing about.

I have used mortality schedules to find the spouse of an ancestor, as well as to find the infant son of a couple whom I had assumed were childless – at least until I found his name on the mortality schedule.

When looking at mortality schedules, note the name and number of the Enumeration District at the top of the census page. Each entry on the Mortality Schedule will list the family *number* to which the deceased belonged. Go to the appropriate Enumeration District on the regular US census page and find the family number. That is the family to which the person who had passed away belonged.

If you have an opportunity to search mortality schedules, you may find it interesting to note the ages of those who died. So many of them are children under age 10 — infant and young child mortality was very high in the mid-1800s. And, in cold weather climates, an inordinate number of young children died between September and April – when colder weather descended. I guarantee it will tug at your heartstrings!

Generally speaking, you'll find each state's mortality schedules wherever you find their federal censuses. Those locations include each state's library and archives, several subscription-based services like Ancestry.com, Heritage Quest, etc., and at the Family History Library of the LDS Church.

Don't overlook Mortality Schedules! They may help find missing ancestors.

British Records

Not to be completely US-centric, I think it bears mentioning that other countries conducted censuses also. Every ten years a census has been conducted in the United Kingdom from 1801 through present day. Unlike US censuses, these were conducted in the *second* year of each decade – 1801, 1811, 1821, and so on. Our neighbors across the pond did not conduct a census in 1941 – they had other things on their minds! A census was also not conducted in Northern Ireland or the Republic of Ireland during 1921 – due to the volatile atmosphere that accompanied the establishment of the Irish Free State the following year.

The UK censuses were similar in many regards to the US censuses. Questions and information gathered are very similar to their cousin US censuses. The earliest censuses taken (1801 to 1841) were only headcount-based. Like the US censuses, questions were added as the years went on.

British census records are available at Ancestry.com as well as FamilySearch.org. To access them on Ancestry.com, you need to have their international subscription.

Immigration & Naturalization Records

For my money, some of the most exciting genealogy records to research are those having to do with immigration and naturalization. The sheer amount of information that can be gleaned from these tremendous records is incredible. Most of us in the US generally don't go back too many generations until we come to an ancestor who immigrated to America. Those who did so were often required to complete very extensive questionnaires that shed a lot of light on their lives as well as information about their spouses, children, and in some cases, parents.

Earlier in this book we covered Ellis Island – in the *Free Services* chapter. As you saw there, great gobs of genealogically relevant information were gleaned from passengers on ships. If you are uncertain where your ancestors arrived in the United States, searching indices and databases that contain the names of immigrants entering through ports should be the first step you take. Use common sense in your search. If your ancestor settled in the Philadelphia area, check indices for the port of Philadelphia. At the same time, don't overlook the nearby port of Baltimore. As mentioned in the *Ellis Island* section of the book, the top ports through which immigrants came to America were:

New York
Boston
Baltimore
Philadelphia
New Orleans
San Francisco

Nearly 30,000,000 million immigrants disembarked in those six ports. This represents around 75% of the immigrants who arrived in America. Checking databases and passenger lists for those ports is a good place to begin. Ancestry.com has many indexed passenger lists, as does Fold3.com and FamilySearch.org. The National Archives (which we'll discuss later) has immigration lists on microfilm from 1820 through 1982, and many of those lists are indexed and available through one of the services listed above.

In *Troubleshooter's Guide to Do-It-Yourself Genealogy*, I shared an example of an ancestor's family I was able to find and trace through the immigration process. One of the surnames in my family tree is Peoples, and they hail from Ireland and Scotland. Consider how excited I was to find information about the following family who was immigrating to America through Ellis Island: Annie Peoples, age 32, and her three sons (Charles, age 6; Andrew, age 5; and William, age 4), born in Ireland but last residing in Clydebank, Scotland. Annie's occupation was listed as being a wife, Charles as being in school.

Annie and her children came through Ellis Island in September 1924. It was very exciting finding this family, but where was the father? He was missing from this little clutch of a family. As I scanned the information Annie provided when answering questions, I discovered (from answers to questions that are not included above) that she said she was joining her husband William, who lived in Bryn Mawr, Pennsylvania — a great clue to finding information about him. The record also told me that Annie was born in Ramelton, County Donegal, Ireland, that her mother's name was Mrs. Jane McGarvey, and that her children were born in Clydebank, Scotland. Great genealogical (albeit secondary source) information!

Reasoning that if Annie came to America through Ellis Island, perhaps her husband did the same. Alas, a search of Ellis Island passenger lists proved me wrong. From living on the east coast, I knew that Bryn Mawr is very close to Philadelphia, another port for trans-Atlantic ships. I decided to see if there were any passenger lists online for a William Peoples who arrived in the US through the port of Philadelphia. Success! Within moments of opening Ancestry.com, I was able to find this information:

William Peoples,
— 35 years old
— laborer
— never been to the US before
— Irish nationality
— residence was Clydebank, Scotland
— spouse: Annie Peoples
— born in Ramelton, Ireland
— final destination: Bryn Mawr, Pennsylvania
— wanted to remain in the US "Always" (meaning he was immigrating and not just visiting)
— his ticket was paid for by his cousin, William Montgomery of Bryn Mawr, Pennsylvania
— he was going to join his cousin William in Bryn Mawr, Pennsylvania
— his complexion was described as "fresh," and he had brown hair and blue eyes.
— he had an identifying mark – a white spot in the pupil of his right eye.

Surely this William Peoples is Annie's husband. (Note: William landed in America, the land of opportunity, with a whole $27 in his pocket!) I also don't want to lose track of this cousin, William Montgomery. Perhaps he was his mother's nephew, and – perhaps Montgomery was his mother's maiden name. Perhaps not, but it is a clue worth researching at some point, so don't lose that clue.

We'll pick up the thread on this family in the Naturalization Records section that follows.

Naturalization Records

Most early immigrants to the United States wanted to become US citizens. To do so, they were required to complete naturalization papers. From the

1790s until the Immigration and Naturalization Act was enacted in 1906, these documents were handled by the individual states. There was little consistency to the records – some states asked for buckets of information, others asked just a few basic questions. In 1906, control of this aspect of the American citizenry came to the federal government, and the processes became much better defined and standardized.

I knew that if I could find William's or Annie's naturalization papers, I would have a wealth of additional information about their family. In their cases, we knew the years they immigrated, so had at least an idea or when they might have first submitted their naturalization papers – five years after they arrived. The earliest William would have been able to submit his papers

NATURALIZATION RECORDS

The basic documents found in the naturalization process are as follows:

Declaration of Intention – Those wishing to become American citizens completed a *Declaration of Intention*, declaring their intention to become an American citizen. Sometimes referred to as *first papers*, they are rich in genealogical data.

Naturalization Petition – Once an immigrant had competed residency requirements (usually five years in the US), they could file a *Naturalization Petition.* These documents asked some of the same genealogical questions as the *Declaration of Intent*, but asked a few other questions that provide value to genealogists. Often referred to as *second papers.*

Oath of Allegiance – Just what it sounds like. It provides a renunciation of their former government / citizenry.

Certificate of Arrival – This short document identifies the date, port of arrival and ship in which the individual arrived.

was in 1928, and in Annie's case, she could have submitted her papers in 1929. I was able to identify those potential dates because I had been able to find William and Annie on passenger lists. Had I not been able to find them on a passenger list, I could have also used US censuses as a clue. The 1900, 1910, 1920 and 1930 censuses asked what year the individual immigrated to the United States. The latter two censuses asked what year they were naturalized.

I tried Ancestry.com to find William's and Annie's naturalization papers, with no luck. I turned to Fold3.com and was rewarded for that effort. I was able to find both his *Declaration of Intent* as well as his *Naturalization Petition.* Here's the information both contained:

Declaration of Intent, November 18, 1926, filed in the Court of Common Pleas of Montgomery County, Pennsylvania

Name – William Peoples
Age – 37
Birth place – Ramelton, County Donegal, Ireland
Birth date – June 1, 1889
Current residence – Ardmore, Pennsylvania
Wife's name – Annie
Wife was born at – Ramelton, County Donegal, Ireland
Port of arrival of immigrant – Philadephia
Date of arrival – April 23, 1923

So I picked up a few additional nuggets of genealogy information – William's birth date and place as well as his wife's birth place. I also know where they were living in 1926, a clue that may help me find other documents about the family.

Petition for Naturalization, filed with the District Court of the United States, Eastern District of Pennsylvania, on February 25, 1929:

Name – William Peoples
Age – 39
Occupation – engineer
Birth place – Ramelton, County Donegal, Ireland
Birth date – June 1, 1889
Current residence – Ardmore, Pennsylvania
Emigrated to the US from – Liverpool, England
Port of arrival of immigrant – Philadephia
Date of departure – April 10, 1923
Date of arrival – April 23, 1923
Vessel – Haverford
Wife's name – Annie
Wife's birth date – July 24, 1891
Wife was born at – Ramelton, County Donegal, Ireland
Number of children – 4
Names, birth dates, birth places and current residence of children:

Charles, April 26, 1917, born Clydebank, Scotland, living in Ardmore, PA

Andrew, October 6, 1918, born Clydebank, Scotland, living in Ardmore, PA

William George, November 6, 1919, born Clydebank, Scotland, living Ardmore, PA

Robert John, June 26, 1925, born in Narberth, PA, living in Ardmore, PA

Even more information was provided on this document, including Annie's birth date, the names, birth dates and places of their children. I knew their children's ages and birth places from the Ellis Island passenger lists, but had

I not had those, this document would have provided even more additional information. Note that they had a child after their arrival in the US.

A search for Annie's naturalization papers was unsuccessful, probably because she just became a citizen by virtue of her husband's citizenship. Before 1922, women and minors didn't have to file naturalization papers; they could become American citizens when their husbands and fathers did.

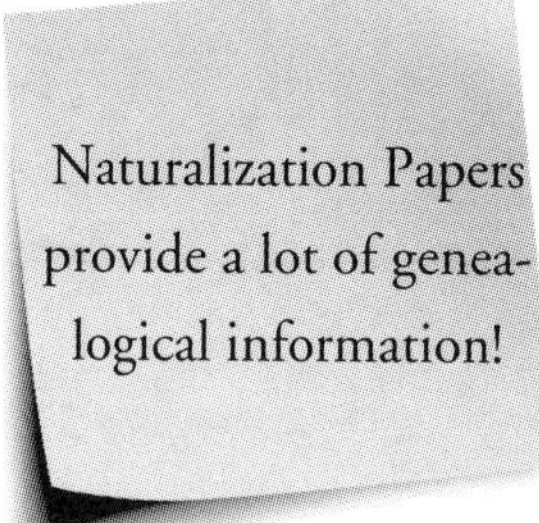
Naturalization Papers
provide a lot of genea-
logical information!

As you can see, immigration and naturalization records can provide a virtual wealth of information and be a great aid in your search for your ancestors. As time goes by, more and more immigration and naturalization records become available online, both through free as well as subscription services.

Birth, Marriage & Death Records

Without a doubt, online birth, marriage and death records are a boon to genealogists. For years, those records were only available through snail mail or personal visits to government offices or libraries in the area where the event occurred. Many of those records have found their way online, a true blessing for genealogists.

Many states have resorted to providing such records through several pay-per-certificate services, such as VitalChek and VitalRec.com, or Archives.com a subscription service ($39.95 per year). Personally, I am not a big fan of the per-certificate services – they are very expensive when compared to other online genealogy services. As we have discussed, many of those services are free, while others charge a subscription fee. But when you consider one record – a birth, marriage or death record – can cost you $15 to $75, depending on the state you are searching, you will begin to think of the Ancestry.coms of the world as bargains! I try very hard to locate these important records through free or other subscription services before succumbing to paying those higher fees.

Having said that, many of those vital records are available online through free services. Try Googling what you are looking for – *Missouri Death Records*, for example. Sometimes states offer two services – one free and one through one of the agencies listed above. Poke around – it's worth your time – to see if you can find what you are looking for without having to pay for it. Often, genealogy societies put such information online. Several of my family lines go back to Schuyler County, Illinois. They have a very active genealogy society, and they have placed a number of records online for use by genealogists. More often than not, records are abstracted or transcribed, rather than showing pictures of the actual certificate or page in birth, marriage or death registry books. For example, here is a partial listing of transcribed birth records from the Schuyler County Genealogy Society:

Schuyler County, Illinois
Birth Records

The following birth records were extracted from FHL Microfilm 1311546. These records were filmed from the original Birth Record books at the Schuyler County Courthouse. The information below lists the child's name, birthdate, birthplace, and parents. It should be noted that the records themselves contain more information than I've chosen to include here. Copies can be obtained from the above mentioned microfilm, the Schuyler County Clerk, or the Schuyler County Historical Jail Museum. Be forewarned: handwriting is subject to interpretation :)

Birth Records, Book 1, 1877-1886, Pages 71 - 77

#	Name	Birth	Mother	Father
	Page 71			
900	female Ray	19 May 1880, Hickory Tp.	Aramintha (Kelly) Ray	Isaac Ray
901	male Ridings	7 Jun. 1880, Woodstock Tp.	Margaret (Paisly) Ridings	James Egbert Ridings
902	Mable Edith Mason	25 Jun. 1880	Ann (Root) Mason	William E. Mason
903	female Davis	16 Jul. 1880, Buenavista Tp.	Hannah Arminda Greene	David G. P. Davis
904	male Hellyar	14 Jul. 1880, Brooklyn	Kate (Dunlavy) Hellyar	Geo. Hellyar
905	male Curtis	17 Jul. 1880, Brooklyn Tp.	Lucinda (Willey) Curtiss	John Curtis
906	Josephine Frakes	7 Jul. 1880, Brooklyn Tp.	Rebecca Jane (Stoneking) Frakes	John Henry Frakes
907	Emma Elizabeth Parsons	10 Jul. 1880, Brooklyn Tp.	Elisabeth C. (Pruett) Parsons	Jacob B. Parsons
908	Thomas Jefferson Powell	8 Jul. 1880, Hickory Tp.	Eliza Jane (Tire) Powell	John Roach Powell
909	Birtha Hollingsworth	19 Jun. 1880, Browning	Laura Amanda (Lancaster) Hollingsworth	Abram Hollingsworth
910	male Baley	[no date], Birmingham	Mary J. (Milton) Baley	John H. Baley
911	Bertha Hanning	24 J [sic] 1880, Birmingham Tp.	Martha P. (Henderson) Hanning	Robert Hanning
	Page 72			
912	Stillo Bates	7 May 1880, Browning Tp.	Agnus (Campbell) Bates	John W. Bates
913	male Allphin	25 Jul. 1880, Huntsville	Atlanta (Wilson) Allphin	George Allphin
914	James Wardell	5 Jul. 1880, Woodstock Tp.	Nancy J. (Robins) Wardell	Francis M. Wardell
915	Frank Moork	16 May 1880, Rushville	Huldah Louisa (Frederickson) Moork	Christian Moork

In the case of the above information, members of the local genealogy society ordered microfilmed pages of vital records from FamilySearch.org, then transcribed the information and put it online. A great service.

Many vital records are kept at the county level, so Googling for records at the county level might yield results. Depending on the county, the records may be free or there may be a cost associated with them.

Through the years, I have found that birth and death records have found their way online more than marriage records have, but recently it seems marriage records are catching up.

Military Records

From the Revolutionary War through World War I, the federal government has kept a wonderful assortment of records on their military men. Even some records were kept for wars/skirmishes prior to the formation of the country: King Philip's War (1675 – 1676), King William's War (1689 – 1697), Queen Anne's War (1702 – 1713) and the French and Indian Wars (1754 – 1763).

Various records are available for the men who served in America's military through the years. Generally speaking, the earlier the service, the less information is available. For example, the pre-Revolutionary War records for service men are pretty much limited to rosters and payroll cards. The Civil War-era records are plentiful and exceptionally rich in genealogical information. World War I and World War II draft registration records also provide excellent information of interest to genealogists.

The following kinds of records are available for your military ancestors:

Bounty Land Warrants – Most people have at least heard of these. In our nation's early days, the federal government often paid their military men with land. Bounty Land Warrants were the vehicles used to do that. Bounty Land Warrants were used between 1766 and 1855.

Enlistment Records – Depending on the war, enlistment records may provide you with a little or a lot of information. Civil War records, especially for the Union side, provide a great deal of genealogically valuable information.

Draft Registration Cards – American men – as well as non-American men living in America – were required to register for the draft during World War I and World War II. Many of the World War II Draft Registration Cards are not yet available due to government privacy laws. However, there was an Old Men's Registration conducted on April 24, 1942 that registered men whose birthdays fell between 28 April 1877 and 16 February 1897. These men were between 45 and 64 years old, and were not currently serving in the military.

Not to be overlooked, there was a draft instituted during the Civil War also, in 1863 on the Union side. Several items of important genealogical information was available through those draft records also.

Records of Events – These records don't have much genealogical value, but are interesting to read. They are like journal entries of the movements of various military units. They would be of interest if you wanted to see what battles your ancestor fought in.

Compiled Military Service Records – These records (called CMSR records) were kept by the Union Army during the Civil War. They include pay rolls, leave requests, muster sheets (roll calls), and other interesting information.

Pension Records – I have had great success finding pension records for a number of my military ancestors. The veterans could have applied, or their widows and/or children. Regardless of who made application, a great deal of genealogically significant information can be gleaned from pension applications.

As pointed out earlier in this book, my third-great grandfather served in the Civil War. I have been able to locate a number of military records – all online — for him, including his enlistment papers, CMSR records and the pension application his wife filed upon his death. Following are the kinds of information I was able to glean from those records:

— his birth date
— his birth place
— his wife's maiden name
— his wife's birth date
— his wife's death date
— date of his marriage
— place of his marriage
— the names and ages of his children who were 16 years of age or younger in May 1863
— his residence
— his occupation
— his physical description
— his place of death
— his death date

His pension application, in particular, was of great value, listing the names and birth dates for each of his children that were age 16 and younger at the time application for a pension was made by his widow.

An important note about Confederate records: The federal government did not issue pensions to members of the confederate army. However, all the states of the Confederacy did. While the National Archives now has these records in their collection, you may want to stop first at the state from which your ancestor served.

Moving from the Civil War to World War I, below is a copy of my great grandfather's World War I Draft Registration Card.

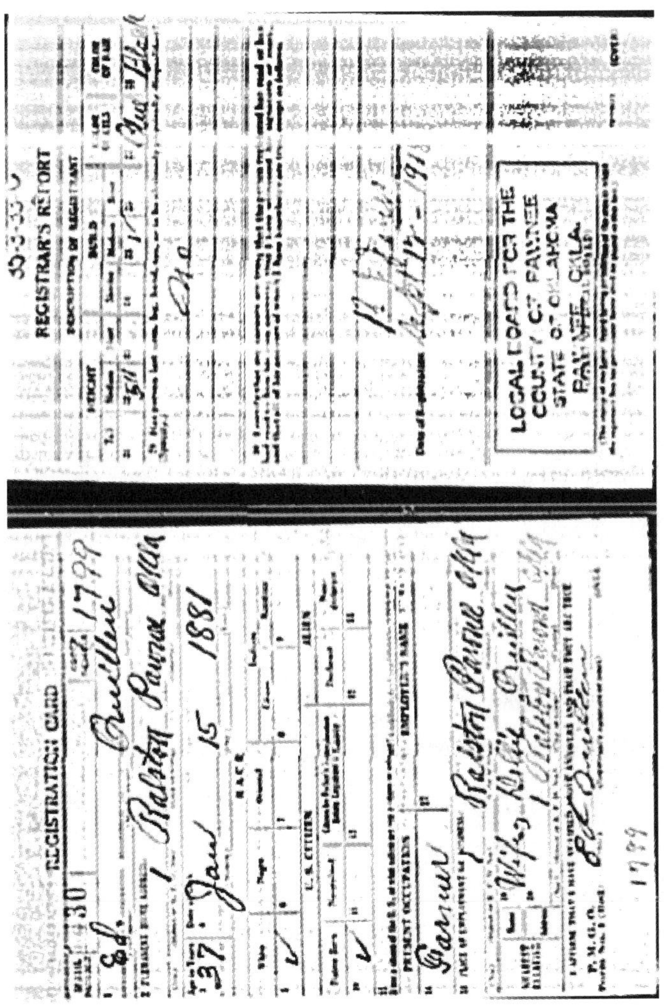

REGISTRATION CARD

REGISTRAR'S REPORT

LOCAL BOARD FOR THE
COUNTY OF PAWNEE
STATE OF OKLAHOMA
PAWNEE, OKLA.

There has been a lot of speculation about my great grandfather's birth date. For many years, the family believed he had been born in 1880. But his birthday is in January, and he did not appear on the census report for 1880, which was enumerated in June. So we just assumed his birthday must have been in 1881. At least for this document, my great grandfather listed his birth date as being in 1881. It's still a secondary source, but it has helped clear up the question of his birth year.

Even the best photocopies of these World War I draft registration records seem to be somewhat blurry, so following are the questions that were asked. There were actually three different registration periods, between June 1917 and September 1918, and while the questions varied somewhat, they generally asked the same questions.

— Name
— Home address
— Age in years
— Birth date
— Birth place
— Birth place of Father
— Race
— Native born, naturalized citizen, *Declaration of Intent* signed, non-citizen or Indian
— Occupation
— Employer's name
— Employer's place of business
— Nearest relative
— Nearest relative's address
— Brief physical description

Each of those questions yields information valuable to a genealogist.

So where does one find such wonderful records? Well, they are available numerous (many!) places on the Internet.

Subscription services like Fold3.com and Ancestry.com have many of the records. Ancestry boasts that they have over 24 million draft registration cards (the full set), while Fold3.com has only around 5,000 (although they are adding all the time). However, at the time of this writing, Fold3.com has announced that they have received a contract from the federal government to begin putting many of the military records held in the National Archives online. Since Fold3.com is now part of the Ancestry.com family, I would expect them to bypass adding draft registration cards (since Ancestry already has them), and focus on other military records that Ancestry doesn't have.

FamilySearch.org also has many of these records also. Some are online, although many are not. For example, they have all 24 million draft registration cards, but thus far, none of them are available online – they are all on microfilm that can be borrowed through visiting any of their 4,300 Family History Centers.

As I mentioned earlier in this book, many local genealogy societies have also put military records online. Realizing the tremendous amount of genealogical information available in the military records, they have focused many of their resources on transcribing the military records for those who are from their own county or town. For example, by Googling *Mifflin County military records*, the first hit I came to was part of the USGenWeb Archives project for Pennsylvania. The very first name listed on the page was Joseph Cunningham – the same name as my third-great grandfather. Clicking on the file provided, I found a transcription of his original Revolutionary War pension application, along with the pension application his wife submitted upon his death. From those two documents, besides learning his rank, regiments and the battles in which he fought, I also learned:

— Joseph's age (born in 1752 or 1753)
— Margaret's age (born in 1760 or 1761)
— the name and age of one daughter who was still living with them (Mary, born 1795)
— Their marriage date (January 31, 1786)
— Place of marriage (Chester Co., Pennsylvania)
— Joseph's death date (August 14, 1838)

National Archives (NARA)

The National Archives (NARA) is one of the most fun genealogy websites to poke around on. To get there, head for *www.archives.gov*. It is a tremendous site for finding genealogical information that is at times exhilarating and at other times disappointing. If it has a down-side, it has so much information. And after spending years and years researching various and sundry nooks and crannies on the website, I can tell you that it isn't the easiest to navigate. But – the information available there is so valuable – whether through inter-library loan or via online digital images, it is well worth your effort to tackle it.

Other sections of this book address specific areas of research within NARA – such as military records, immigration and naturalization records, etc. Let's just take a tour of the website so that you are comfortable with it. So, type in *www.archives.gov* (*www.archives.com* is a subscription service, so make sure you type *.gov* instead of *.com*!).

PHOTOGRAPHER
SUPERIOR STREET
CLEVELAND, O.

On the home page, you'll note a number of tantalizing places to click, but let's stay focused. On the left side, near the bottom, you'll see a section entitled *Information For*, and underneath that several options. *Genealogists* is one of your choices. Click on that.

Doesn't this page just make your genealogist's heart sing:

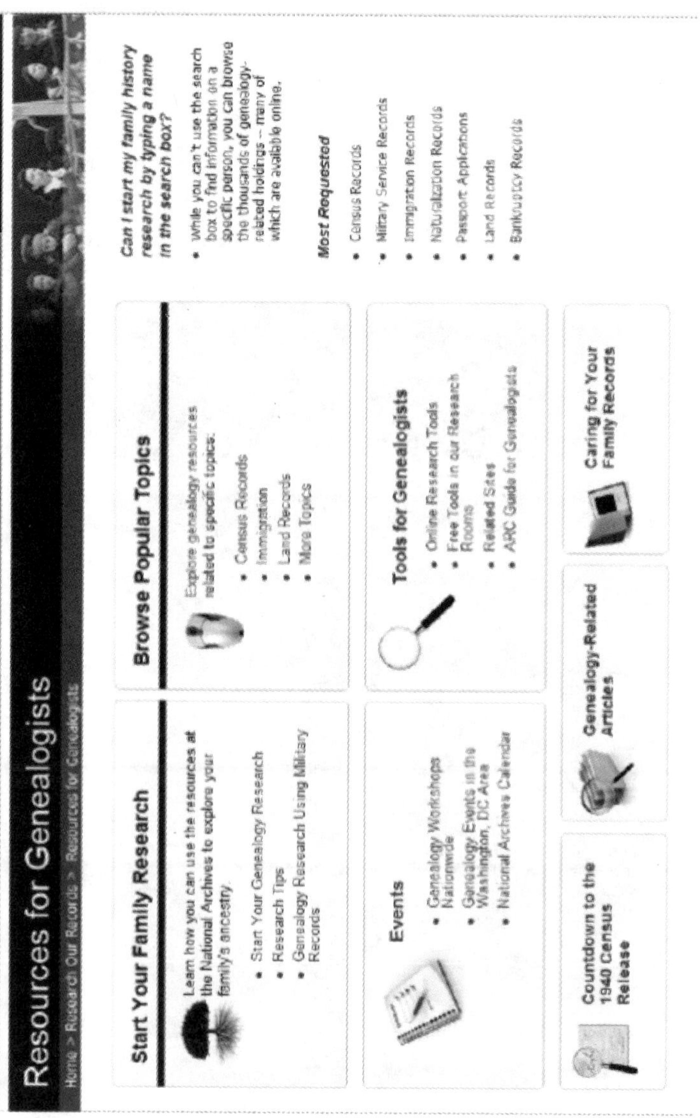

I like the *Browse Popular Topics* section in the center of the page. The first item listed under that is *Census Records* (that's the exhilaration part!). Click on *Census Records*, and the first thing you'll see is the sentence, "We do not have census records on the National archives web site." (And there is the disappointment!). They quickly advise you that they do have microfilm catalogs available online. They also advise that online census records are available through Ancestry.com and HeritageQuest.com.

Back to the page you were on before, you'll note some other areas on the right-hand side – the *Most Requested* documents. As you read through those, you'll see that someplace in the narrative you are told that they have few of those items online (they must get a LOT of requests!). They are microfilmed, and can be seen by identifying the specific films you wish to see and then finding out if those particular films are at one of the regional National Archives Centers nearest you. Regional centers are located in:

— Anchorage, Alaska
— Laguna Niguel, California
— San Bruno, California
— Denver, Colorado
— East Point, Georgia
— Chicago, Illinois
— Waltham, Massachusetts
— Pittsfield, Massachusetts
— New York, New York
— Philadelphia, Pennsylvania
— Fort Worth, Texas
— Seattle, Washington
— Washington DC

Sure wish the federal government would put their records online!

Suffice it to say, the federal government has many records in their collections. As of this writing, many are difficult to get to unless you travel to Washington DC or live near a regional archives center. But slowly, portions of their collections are coming online – usually through subscription services. We can only hope that in years' to come, all the federal government's genealogy records will be available online.

Wills & Probate Records

Wills are the documents used by families and the government to disburse an individual's assets upon his or her death. Finding the will of a deceased ancestor can be an enlightening experience. It can be enlightening genealogically because you may learn the names of your ancestor's spouse and children. You may also learn their ages and perhaps even their married names and the names of their spouses. It can be enlightening to learn the amount of property (or lack thereof) that an ancestor possessed at his or her death, and sometimes even the value of that property.

Testate = the person who died left a will. **Intestate** = the person who died did not leave a will.

Every state has laws that require that the estates of deceased persons must be handled through the courts, whether the person left a will or not. The titles of the officials who oversee the probate process vary by jurisdiction, and may be called probate judges, city, county or district judges, town or county clerks or registrars of wills.

Probate records are the court records covering the final disposition of an individual's assets upon his or her death.

Wills and probate records are slowly becoming more and more available online. Perhaps not as plentiful as censuses or military records, they are nonetheless becoming more available. I have had luck finding them in a number of places, including RootsWeb, Ancestry.com, FamilySearch.org, Cyndi's List, USGenweb and Fold3.com.

And, not to sound like a broken record, be sure and check out local genealogy societies to see if they have transcribed (copied word-for-word) or abstracted (summarized) wills and probate records from the area where your ancestor lived. These are popular activities for the members of local genealogy societies, because wills and probate records often yield so much valuable information for genealogists.

8. GENEALOGY SOFTWARE REVIEWS

In two of my other genealogy books, *Secrets of Tracing Your Ancestors* and *Troubleshooter's Guide to Do-It-Yourself Genealogy*, I have extensive reviews on genealogy software. Since this book deals with online genealogy, and presumably you will be using software to store all the genealogical information you find, I will visit briefly some of the top genealogy software on the market today. For a more in-depth look, however, you might check out either of the books mentioned above.

Personal Ancestral File – PAF for short – has been the foundation and standard for genealogy software for years. Produced by the LDS Church, it is provided for free to those who wish to have it.

PAF allows you to collect and record information about birth, baptism, marriage, death and burial dates for each individual. In addition, each event allows you to enter notes regarding the source of information, or just about anything you would like to add.

While PAF has been the standard around which all (or at least most!) other genealogy softwares rallied, the LDS Church announced it would no longer provide PAF as a free download, nor would they support it any longer. So – if you have PAF (I still use it), be aware that it is no longer supported, and is no longer available for download.

Family Tree Maker is one of the newer entrants into the genealogy software market, and they have a fine product. As of this writing, the cost is just south $40 ($39.95), but can sometimes be gotten on sale for close to $30. Affiliated with Ancestry.com, Family Tree Maker provides a rich set of features and capabilities. One of the best features of this package, I think, is its ability to link photos to specific ancestors.

Ancestral Quest was once one of the leaders in the genealogy software market, but they have lagged in recent years. However – it's still a terrific and very viable product. Recent prices for Ancestral Quest were in the $29.95 range.

I like the intuitive feel Ancestral Quest has – it is easy to learn and navigate. Like Family Tree Maker, you can attach photos, audio and video clips, a nice thing to be able to do if you have information captured like that.

RootsMagic is another software package in the $29.95 range, like Ancestral Quest. And like Ancestral Quest, it is software that is easy to learn for beginners, but it also has enough power and functionality for much more advanced genealogists. Users of RootsMagic swear by it, and you can't pry it out of their hands. It's also Vista compatible, and that makes a lot of genealogists smile.

Try some of the free trials to see which genealogy software works best for my needs.

RootsMagic comes with a series of free downloads and trials, so you can take it for a test drive to see if you like it.

The last software package I'll mention is **Legacy Family Tree**. Like some of the other software packages listed here, it is user-friendly and easy to learn.

They offer video training packages as part of their software for those who learn visually – a nice option.

With Legacy Family Tree, you can add photographs, sound and video clips to your family records. It also has a web page creation capability. It's a lot of fun to play around with, and should provide you with all the horsepower you'll need for awhile as you do your genealogical research.

The standard edition of Legacy Family Tree is free, and upgraded packages run from $29.95 to $59.95, depending on the version and documentation / training materials you want to order.

9. GLOSSARY

Blog – short for Web Log, an online journal or "log" kept and generally shared with the public, or a close group of friends and family.

Browser – a method for accessing the World Wide Web (www.....)

Bulletin Board – see also Message Board. A place where you can go online to seek and share information; in this context – genealogy information.

Database – a collection of information that can be searched in many ways – by name, date of birth, birth place, etc.

E-mail – Electronic Mail. A communication medium very popular with genealogists, who send messages from their computer to another's computer. Delivery is generally more or less instantaneous.

Family Group Sheet – a collection of genealogical information about an individual, usually grouped with his or her family (parents, spouse, children).

Flame – to "light up" another person with a rude, sarcastic or unkind comment or comments, generally in electronic format – such as e-mail or on a message board.

GEDCOM – acronym for **GE**nealogical **D**ata **COM**munication. The standard protocol and format for transferring genealogy information electronically between software packages.

LDS – common acronym for the Latter-day Saints, more formally known as The Church of Jesus Christ of Latter-day Saints, more informally known as the Mormon Church.

Listserv – an e-mail group of individuals with a common interest (in this case – genealogy or a particular surname).

Message Board — see also Bulletin Board. A place where you can go online to seek and share information; in this context – genealogy information.

Pedigree Chart – a chart that linearally shows the ancestry of an individual, from himself or herself back from one generation to the next.

Personal Ancestry File – also known as PAF, a free genealogy software produced for many years by the LDS Church. It is no longer available nor is it supported. But it still works if you have it!

Primary Source – genealogy records created at the time of the event. A birth certificate would be considered an primary source for birth date and birth place.

Search Engine – a program used to search the World Wide Web for information and data.

Secondary Source – genealogy records where information is provided much later than the event. A tombstone or death certificate would be considered a primary source for death information, but a secondary source for birth information, since it is likely that the birth information was provided many years after the person's birth occurred.

Social Networking – any of hundreds of software applications that allows people to get together online and share information – often of a social nature. Some of the more common social networking applications are Facebook, Twitter and MySpace.

Social Security Death Index – a database of individuals who had social security numbers and who have died. Individuals can search for anyone in this database who died between the 1960s and present day. Some genealogical information can be gleaned from this site.

URL – also called universal resource locator, or uniform resource locator. This is the address of a website. Most often it will start with *http://www.* – although sometimes the www is not included in the address.

Vital Records – this is the term used to identify documents that contain information about an individual's birth, marriage and death.

WIKI – a website that provides information on some individual or topic. As it relates to genealogy, it may be set up to assist with research of a particular family surname, region or country.

INDEX